OREGON
Aviation

OREGON
★ ★ *Aviation* ★ ★
A DARING HISTORY

Arthur H. Redman

THE
History
PRESS

Published by The History Press
Charleston, SC
www.historypress.com

First published 2025

Manufactured in the United States

ISBN 9781467157421

Library of Congress Control Number: 2024944900

CONTENTS

INTRODUCTION

The history of aviation in Oregon and the Pacific Northwest is the same as any other American state. First comes the launching of balloons using smoke that is heated air as a buoyant or lifting force, invented in France by the Gondolier brothers in 1789. Hydrogen balloons in the American Civil War served as aerial spies on Confederate troops, aiding Oregon's Senator Edward D. Baker, who commanded troops around Washington, D.C., in 1861 and Yorktown, where Lieutenant John Lingenfelter from Jacksonville, Oregon, was stationed as a picket.

In 1868, a newspaper reported that a Salem, Oregon resident build a model of a helicopter. The overhead rotor blades of the machine were hand powered by a crank and did not run by steam, compressed air or electricity.

The first balloon ascension in Oregon took place in 1868 at Albany. More balloons and aeronauts arrived in Oregon in the form of Park Van Tassel, Professor P.H. Redmond and other performers who traveled to Oregon during the 1880s. Plans for airships by Oregonians Captain J.W. Kern, E.W. Dixon and E.F. Debort appeared in 1890s newspapers like wild schemes by people trying to raise capital for dubious designs.

Octave Chanute, author of *Progress in Flying Machines*, wrote in 1893 about an idealized vision of a flying machine that it "will bring nothing but good into the world; that it will abridge distance, make all parts of the globe accessible, bring men into closer with each other advance civilization, and hasten the promise era which there shall be nothing but peace and good-will among all men."

No wonder men of the Pacific Northwest and elsewhere strove to perfect their aviation designs. Grant Keys, a mechanic and railroad man from Elgin, Oregon, designed kites and launched gliders. Keys and his assistant assessed sizes and shapes of kites on the slopes of Mount Emily and the hill adjacent to Morgan Lake, elevation 4,154 feet, north of Morgan Lake Road, where he attempted a powered flight during 1904.

The first controlled flight in Oregon featured a hydrogen-filled powered balloon or directional balloon, a dirigible as the French called it or airship according to the Germans; it ascended over the Lewis and Clark Exposition grounds in 1905. It was constructed by Thomas Baldwin and powered by a five-horsepower one-cylinder engine and was steered left or right by a moveable vertical surface, the rudder. Later in the 1920s and 1930s, three famous helium-filled dirigibles or rigid-frame airships—the *Shenandoah*, *Macon* and *Akron*—flew over cities of the Pacific Northwest but had no lasting influence on aviation.

An airplane is not an airship and has no buoyant force of its own. It does not float in the air but rather is driven through it by a gas engine and is heavier than air. Keels are fixed surfaces exerting no lifting effect or rudder action, while the "supporting planes" or wings are the main lifting surface of the airplane, as distinguished from all auxiliary or stabilizing surfaces. The movable vertical surface steering the craft up or down is the "elevation rudder." The movable horizontal surface, the "directional rudder," steers the craft left or right. Airplanes also have devices for "transverse control," used for the preservation of lateral balance in wind gusts and artificial inclination when making turns.

The first extended airplane flight was achieved by the Wright brothers when Wilbur flew 852 feet during their fourth flight of that memorable day December 17, 1903. The first airplane to fly in Oregon was on March 5, 1910, a Curtiss biplane piloted by Charles Hamilton and purchased by Portland automobile dealer Henry Wemme. The first plane constructed and flown in Oregon was built by John Burkhart, who flew it at Albany one month later. Deliveries began in 1912, to Vancouver, Washington, flown by Silas Christofferson and Walter Edwards.

"They are putting their lives in the balance every time they go aloft," said Portland aviation backer Fred Bennett about flyers. "I don't want anyone's blood on my hands."

It's tragic how scores of the early aviators who flew in Oregon died in crashes before 1921. It is also remarkable that Charles Hamilton, who made the first plane flight in Oregon, died a natural death at age twenty-three. John Burkhart, the first Oregonian to build and fly his own plane, retired from flying in 1912 because of a promise he made to his wife to give up the practice. Other aviators were not so fortunate—Eugene Ely and Charles Walsh crashed in 1911, Thomas Baldwin and Lincoln Beachey in 1915 at San Francisco, Silas Christofferson in 1916, Louis Barin in an airplane collision in 1920 at San Diego and John "Tex" Rankin at Klamath Falls in 1947. Female aviators from Oregon and Washington are also of importance in this narrative.

Aircraft manufacturing companies were formed in the Pacific Northwest. The Portland firm Rekar Company hoped to make a powered balloon or directional balloon. Airplane manufacturing companies included Pacific Aviation in Portland and Boeing of Seattle, along with the corporate mergers of United, Boeing and Pacific Transport. In Washington County, Oregon, the Long Airplane Works and Charles Bernard started the homebuilt plane industry.

Then there was the need for airplane landing fields. Eastmoreland was the first in Portland, dating from 1919, and then came Guild's Lake, Rankin Field and Swan Island in 1927; Pearson in Vancouver; Pounder Field at Parkrose; and Beaverton, Salem, Corvallis, Albany and the Sand Point Naval Station in Seattle.

This aviation history of Oregon ends in 1942 during America's involvement in World War II. The Northwest Air District Headquarters was located at Felts Field near Spokane. Three Oregon aviators were in the fight: two on Jimmy Doolittle's raid on Tokyo and a Flying Tiger born in Yamhill County flying against the Japanese air force in Myanmar (Burma). Other Doolittle raiders searched for Japanese submarines off the Pacific Coast during 1942.

Oregonians were combatants during the Japanese naval and air attack on Dutch Harbor on June 3–4. American bombers based in the Andreanof Islands 125 miles east of Kiska and Attu in the Aleutian Island group began bombing missions on October 8, 1942, liberating them the next year.

CHAPTER I

THE CIVIL WAR ERA, 1861–1882

A writer on the eve of Abraham Lincoln's inauguration said that the capital "had begun to smell like McClellan's new gas balloons." Balloons, other than the hot air variety, employ a reservoir of lighter-than-air gas of either heated air, hydrogen or coal gas to give the aircraft a lifting force. The free balloon becomes part of the wind, moves with the wind, offers no resistance to the wind and floats peacefully as if were a dead calm. If the aeronaut strikes a match to light his cigar, the flame curls straight upward as if he were in a closed room. The pilot has no idea whether the balloon is standing still or moving at forty miles per hour.

Hydrogen-filled balloons, launched by Thaddeus Lowe, aided Oregon senator Edward D. Baker in gaining intelligence on Confederate positions just before his death at the Battle of Ball's Bluff (or Edward Ferry) on October 12, 1861. Earlier on the ground, Captain James Lingenfelter, a resident of Jacksonville, Oregon, was killed near Yorktown under the eyes of Union aerial observers on September 21, 1861.

Thaddeus Sobleski Constantine Lowe became the chief of aerial spying on August 2, 1861, at the age of twenty-nine. The topographical engineers hired Lowe—who stood over six feet tall and had blue eyes, thick black hair and an auburn mustache—to construct and operate a new spy balloon, the *Union*, at a cost of $1,500; it made its first ascent on July 27, 1861, to view Confederate camps at Fairfax, Virginia.

One monster balloon at the center of Massachusetts Avenue and Third Street was in view of a large crowd gathering in Washington, D.C. The balloon was made of oiled linen, thirty-five feet in height from the basket to the top. James Allen was a member of the Rhode Island artillery and moved the balloon to the camp of the Rhode Island regiment near Glenwood. An aeronautical engineer, he was assigned to make aerial observations of Confederate camps and movement.

Allen reported to the U.S. Signal Corps officer Major Albert Meyer by portable field telegraph, which was a combination receiver and telegraph contained in a walnut case about ten by twelve by fourteen inches and which included a handle and a shoulder strap. Electric power was provided by a magneto with a hand crank, which eliminated the need for fresh batteries.

Lowe's balloons were not free flying but rather were anchored by ropes and communicated with the ground crew by either wire telegraph or flags. On the evening of July 11, 1861, Lowe met President Lincoln and offered to perform a demonstration with his balloon, the *Enterprise*, and a telegraph set from a height of five hundred feet above the White House. Lowe telegraphed, "I have the pleasure of sending you this, the first telegraph dispatch ever telegraphed from an aerial station."

Thaddeus Lowe sent another air-to-ground telegram from the balloon on July 18, 1861, during a field demonstration staged for the Union military at the nation's capital. It read: "To President United States: This point of observation commands an area fifty miles in diameter. The city with its girdles of encampments presents a superb scene. I have pleasure in sending you this first dispatch ever telegraphing from an aerial station and in acknowledging indebtedness to your encouragement for the opportunity of demonstrating the availability of science aeronautics in the military service of the country. T.S.C. Lowe."

If the balloon pilot did not ascend with a telegraph operator, the aeronaut drafted his reports while on the ground after landing, and they were taken by a messenger on horseback to the commanding general. Reports written while airborne were attached to a ring and slid down an anchor cable. For lower elevations, the air spy wrapped the paper around a stone and dropped it to the ground or shouted down to a messenger or telegraph operator.

For long-distance signaling, Lowe experimented with mirrors, flags, smaller hot air balloons carrying colored flares and even markings on their envelopes to communicate aerial reports directly from the balloon. Army officers did not have telegraph lines strung to battlefield locations, and balloon reports often took too long to deliver, proving them almost useless to commanders in the field stationed miles away from areas of conflict.

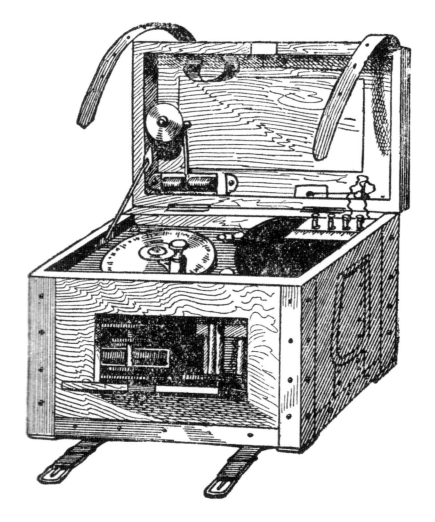

Magneto electric signal telegraph. *From* The Eyes and Ears of the Civil War *(1963), author's copy.*

Lowe demonstrated on September 24, 1861, the use of balloons in aiming artillery from one thousand feet elevation at Fort Corcoran. If firing were to commence to the right of Falls Church, Virginia, Lowe raised a white flag in the balloon, observed by gunners through field glasses. Lowering the flag signaled fire to the left. If over the target, the flag was stationary, and if under, Lowe waved the flag occasionally.

The Army of the Potomac during late September 1861 officially hired Lowe at ten dollars per day as "Chief Aeronaut to the Army of the United States."

Lowe hired ten aeronauts and assistants for the newly minted Balloon Corps, including William Paullin, John La Mountain, John Starkweather, John Steiner (a German), Ebenezer Seaver, Jacob Feno and James Allen. They remained classified as civilian contract employees, receiving five dollars per day; it was a dangerous position if captured because they could be treated as spies and summarily executed.

Lowe and Allen ascended with Lieutenant George Armstrong Custer and other officers, mapmakers and engineers because the army brass did not trust civilians to give reliable reports. General Joseph Hooker ascended in balloons during the Siege of Yorktown and knew the value of aerial reconnaissance firsthand.

"US General A.B. Burnside." Engraving. *From* The Eyes and Ears of the Civil War *(1963), author's copy.*

A telegraph wire, attached to telegraph sounder, directed fire to Union artillery crews on the ground from balloons sent aloft at Fortress Monroe. Messages were either "Too short," "Just a little over, "Fire lower" or "The Last shot took them." The Confederate troops were out of sight of Union artillery gunners. Meanwhile, John Lingenfelter, a volunteer from Oregon, was a picket on the land below in view of Union spy balloons.

Captain James W. Lingenfelter, Company B, was a lawyer from Jacksonville, Oregon. He joined the volunteer 71st Pennsylvania Regiment headed by Oregon's Senator Edward D. Baker. He served as a picket near Lewinsville, Virginia, where on September 21, 1861, at the age of twenty-four, he was shot in the head by a Confederate sniper while on picket duty. He had left the pickets and, together with a sergeant, advanced into the wood, off the Kirby Road, on a reconnoitering patrol when they were surrounded.

Senator Baker of Oregon telegraphed the news to Jacksonville, Oregon, days before he himself was killed at the Battle of Ball's Bluff; it was published in the *Jacksonville Sentinel* of October 26, 1861. Colonel Baker wrote of Lingenfelter to a resident: "During his short military career, he evinced superior capacity and has left behind him no man of more promise, and indeed the only fault with him was that his boiling courage scorned the caution inseparable from a perfect soldier. While I regret that the state of Oregon is called on to deplore the loss of an excellent, I rejoice that she has many more that will offer their best blood in defense of a constitution and form a government which are the only guarantees of civil and religious liberty."

One of the early aeronauts was Lieutenant George Armstrong Custer, who fifteen years later met his demise at the Battle of the Little Bighorn. General Fritz John Porter told Custer "to take with me in my balloon ascent a field glass, compass, pencil, and note-book. I was supposed to be able, after attaining the proper elevation, to discover, locate, and record the works and encampments of the enemy. The balloon was kept but a short distance from General Smith's headquarters, like a wild and untamable animal."

Custer observed the "York River, following with the eye could rest on Chesapeake Bay. On the left and at about the same distance flowed the James River….Between these two rivers extended a more beautiful landscape, and no less interesting than beautiful…Yorktown, which could be seen in the far distance, as it rested on the right bank of the York River."

East and west flowed the Potomac River. Toward the east lies the nation's capital, which was not visible to Custer from the balloon at one thousand feet—the usual altitude held due to ropes or men on the ground. However, he could see where Lieutenant John Lingenfelter from Jacksonville, Oregon, served as picket near Yorktown. Lingenfelter was the first Oregonian to die in combat during the American Civil War.

The bluffs twenty-five miles east of Washington, D.C., is the location where Senator Edward D. Baker of Oregon lost his life at the Battle of Ball's Bluff in Virginia, viewed by Union balloons. John Starkweather took with him in the balloon a field glass, compass, pencil and notebook. With these he was supposed to be able, after attaining the proper elevation, to discover, locate and record the works and encampments of the enemy. In an open country, a balloon became valuable in locating any Confederate camps and trenches, but unfortunately for aerial spies, army camps were also pitched in the forests and woods to avoid the heat of the summer sun.

The forests also concealed Southern earthworks so it became necessary for an aeronaut to attain an altitude of one thousand feet or more and then secure a position directly above the terrain to be examined. With the assistance of a good telescope, it was possible to examine the horizon up to thirty miles away and look for tents through openings in the woods.

The dim outline of an earthwork was just visible, more than half concealed by the trees that have been purposely left standing. Mounted guns were observed, peering sullenly through the embrasures, while men in considerable numbers were standing in and around the entrenchments, often in groups, intently observing the balloon. No one doubted the value of

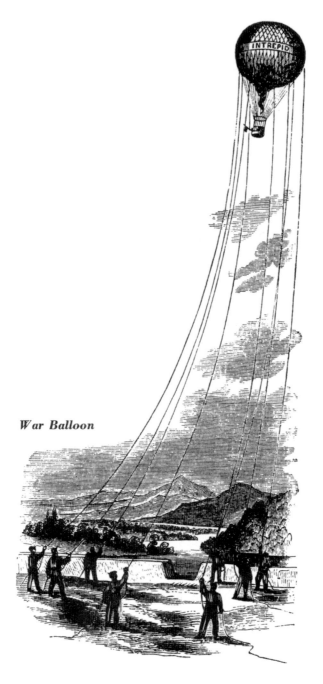

War Balloon

"Civil War Balloon." *From* The Eyes and Ears of the Civil War *(1963),* *author's copy.*

military intelligence gained by the observers peering from their high perch. Creative Southerners painted logs black, making them appear as cannons, called "Quaker guns."

The balloons of the American Civil War era contained hydrogen gas, manufactured by mobile gas generators. The Union army's inflation method, under the direction of Lowe and John Starkweather, proved so effective that they constructed the first aircraft carrier from a converted coal barge, the *George Washington Park Curtis*, carrying two hydrogen generators and two new balloons. One of the balloons, the *George Washington*, was launched off Yorktown at Budd's Ferry, Maryland, on the Potomac River during March 1861. Lowe wrote in a military report, "I have the pleasure of reporting the complete success of the first balloon expedition by water ever attempted."

The chemicals used in balloon inflation are hazardous because hydrogen is highly flammable. The balloons were therefore positioned away from army tents and campfires. In one instance, spilled acid ate through the anchor rope, causing the balloon *Intrepid*, staffed by Union general Fitz John Porter, to ascend unexpectedly. The *Intrepid* danced for an hour above the lines of the Confederate army near Yorktown, Virginia, where Rebels took potshots at the balloon, which was too high to be hit, before it drifted back toward Yankee territory.

Fortunately, Porter knew what to do. He calmly pulled the valve cord, and the hydrogen gas hissed through the open valve at the top of the *Intrepid*. The deflated silk balloon became a parachute, breaking Porter's descent to the ground, where James Allen, along with Lowe's ground crew, rescued the general from Confederate capture.

The value of aerial spying was appreciated by Union general George Stoneman, who said that he "never made an ascent without coming down much better informed than I could have been by any other means." McClellan wrote in his official report, "To Professor Lowe, the intelligent and enterprising aeronaut, who had the management of the balloons, I was greatly indebted for the valuable information obtained during his ascension."

General Lee commented, "The balloons are in constant observation, as expecting or watching movement on our part." Spy balloons made Confederate soldiers anxious. One man wrote to his uncle in North Carolina that he could "see a man up in a balloon every day viewing our camps and we suppose they intend advancing." Colonel E.P. Alexander, head of the Confederate artillery, said that Lowe's "immense black, captive balloons, like two great spirits of the air" were seen by Southern soldiers as they moved north.

Lowe moved to California in 1867, giving up ballooning, waiting for a new lightweight engine other than steam. He became rich inventing a method of making ice before the availability of kitchen refrigerators and a cheaper way to make gas for homes. His greatest dream of crossing the Atlantic Ocean by balloon failed until August 1978, when the helium-filled balloon *Double Eagle II* made the first successful trip in six days from Presque Isle, Maine, flying above Ireland eastward to Paris, France.

Hydrogen-filled balloons never made it to the Pacific Northwest despite Lowe's invention of mobile hydrogen generators, which had advantages over the old process of producing hydrogen gas by pouring sulfuric acid into a tank containing fine iron filings and water. The first ascension of a warm air balloon in Oregon took place at Albany on October 30, 1866, achieved by aeronaut and aerial performer Eustay Buislay of San Francisco.

John Wise contributed to aviation science before he died in a balloon accident, drowning in Lake Michigan on September 29, 1879. He had invented the balloon rip panel in 1839, removing the danger of a balloon being dragged on the ground by a strong wind. He introduced domestic muslin as a balloon material instead of expensive silk, allowing more aeronauts to afford the expense of flying.

Wise discovered that a wide-mouth balloon that flared out inside the netting also served as a parachute, the balloon gently floating to the ground. His book *Through the Air*, published in 1873 a few years before he drowned in Lake Michigan, became a landmark work on balloon science, and it was available to Pacific Northwest readers interested in ballooning.

The great balloonists of the late 1800s made no significant contributions in the way of technical improvements. The designs and patents before 1900 were granted to men who had little or no practical experience in aeronautics. Portland, Oregon, also had such aeronautic designers as Captain J.W. Kern and E.F. De Bort. However, the story of the lost Arctic balloon flight of 1897 by S.A. Andre from Sweden enthralled two young Albany, Oregon aviators, John C. Burkhart and William Crawford, who soon built Oregon's first airplane at Albany.

Inadequate finances were another reason for failure. The cost estimates placed on aircraft designs were much too high for one individual's income to sustain. Also, the expense of additional experimenting necessary to perfect the aircraft added to the strain. In France, a $40,000 grant was made available to the inventors Renard and Krebs, while in the United States, every effort to obtain support from the federal government failed.

It was heated air and coal gas that filled the first balloons in Oregon during the 1880s and not Lowe's generators. Ballooning had become so popular nationwide by 1890 that the president of the Drain Natural Gas Company said that Albany, Oregon, "would be a great town for [a] balloonist as their airships could be inflated at small expense." The first known aeronaut to arrive in Oregon was Park A. Van Tassel, who came to Salem in 1883.

CHAPTER 2

THE BALLOON ERA, 1882–1895

PARK A. VAN TASSEL, 1853?–1930

There were scores of aeronauts active after the American Civil War. There was a demand for aerial entertainment at many festive occasions throughout America. Balloonists were willing to risk their lives to satisfy the public. Ballooning had become a common occupation, reaching the hands of men of slight scientific urges who mostly occupied themselves with balloons to make money, content to make their scheduled public exhibitions all without wanting to investigate the possibilities and the future of heavier-than-air aircraft.

Captain Thomas Scott Baldwin of San Francisco, after his ascents in balloons and making the first parachute jump in the United States, devised a daring specialty of parachute jumping from balloons in 1885. Baldwin toured the country, holding on to the ring of his dangling chute while he ascended in a sitting position on a small seat, swinging his feet over the crowds below. At one thousand feet, Baldwin would pull a rip panel in his balloon (invented by John Wise in 1839) to speed up his fall before jumping to fill the parachute.

Park A. Van Tassel was called "Professor" by aeronauts and piano players in saloons in the 1880s. He was a former bartender born in Albuquerque, New Mexico, around 1853, and he made his first major balloon flight there on June 4, 1882. After the inflation completed, he hoped to take his balloon

NEXT SUNDAY, MARCH 30,

The most daring balloon ascension ever witnessed in East Portland will be given by Miss Adelin Onzalo, direct from Sydney, Australia. She has the reputation of being very clever at this perilous art, and has visited every part of the globe with her sensational performance. Professor Redmond will accompany the lady, who is noted for his fearless and safe ascension. Both parties will perform on the trapeze while the balloon sails majestically above the clouds. Take Jefferson street ferry.

From the Oregonian, *September 7, 1889.*

to the Oregon State Fair grounds, where there was another ascension planned for Saturday, September 22, 1883. The Salem Gas Company was not able to furnish the required supply of gas for the balloon, and the flight scheduled for September 26 was also canceled.

On Saturday, October 20, 1883, Van Tassell arrived in Corvallis, Oregon, after six successful attempts elsewhere in his balloon, the *City of Salt Lake*. His wife accompanied him, agreeing for the first time to make a trip above the clouds. He planned to inflate his thirty-thousand-cubic-foot balloon with coal gas from the gas main extending to the mental health facility building in Corvallis. Advertising ran in the *Oregonian* on October 19–29, 1883, for ascensions in Portland. Accompanied by the editor of the *New Northwest*, Van Tassell ascended successfully on November 5, 1883.

Van Tassell made the first balloon ascent in Washington Territory at Seattle in 1887 and returned to Portland the next year. He failed to ascend on September 24, 1888, because a young bystander, Charles Murphy, became tangled up in the rope. The balloon went up fifteen feet after Van Tassell jumped, and young Charles fell into the Willamette River. The balloon zoomed skyward and was recovered northwest of Lake Oswego.

The balloon inflation occurred at the foot of Montgomery Street, the gas coming from pipes transported to a barge near the Smith Brothers Mill and shipped upriver to City View Park. His wife never made a parachute jump in Oregon as planned due to the lack of gas. The 225-pound Van Tassell finally ascended on a cloudless day to a half mile on October 14, 1888, at 4:00 p.m., viewed by a crowd estimated between 1,200 and 1,500 people.

The balloon darted northward, and then a wind from the northwest drove Van Tassell and his journalist passenger southeast into fleecy white clouds. Forty-five minutes later, the balloon was visible five miles east of Milwaukie. They landed at Rock Creek, eleven miles east of Portland. Van Tassell returned to Portland at 9:45 p.m. and stated that the balloon reached five thousand feet after emerging into sunshine, where expansion of the air inside the balloon took place and he was able to land without mishap.

Van Tassell lived in Seattle for two months, trying to raise money for a new balloon. The original balloon was purchased by N. Hodgeson at a bankruptcy auction held in Portland on November 13, 1888, for $103. The balloon was kept in storage for more than a year in a depot on 35 North Front Street and later sold for rags.

In a newspaper article, it was said that Van Tassell was "Devoured by Sharks" in Honolulu's harbor on November 24, 1889. His wife never believed the reports because she knew that her husband could swim and gave up all parachuting. The victim was actually Joe Lawrence of Albuquerque, New Mexico, hired by Van Tassell to perform all the parachute jumps even though he could not swim.

Van Tassell appeared at Chehalis, Washington, after living eleven years in India. He was hired to ascend there on July 4, 1913.

EDDIE AND THE PROFESSOR

Professor P.H. Redmond, the renowned balloonist and trapeze performer, arrived in Portland, Oregon, during August 1889 with his balloon, which was purchased in Cincinnati, Ohio. The professor was brought to town by Fred T. Merrill, who made his first ascent to one thousand feet on August 15 in his balloon *Chart of the Skies*. The *Oregonian* stated that the balloon exhibition "fully demonstrated the fact Mr. Redmond is a master in his line."

The next two ascensions proved otherwise. P.H. Redmond had to discard his shoes to swim ashore when his balloon landed suddenly in the Willamette River on September 1; he drifted to a nearby log boom. John Enis, a local barber, also landed in the river when he fell from a wharf on the east side of the Willamette while viewing the descent.

The public wanted more, but a strong north wind blew the next day, making it difficult to inflate the air bag via a continuous flame forcing

"Eddie Hall Ascension." Drawing. *From the* Oregonian, *February 12, 1959.*

heated air into the neck. Extreme caution was taken to prevent the sides of the bag from catching fire whenever the wind blew the bag sideways over the mouth of the furnace.

Three thousand people gathered to watch the ascension around 3:00 p.m. from the east side at the Jefferson Street Ferry launch site. Around 6:00 p.m., the professor finally called for help to hold down the balloon. Among those there to help was twelve-year-old Eddie Hall. The trapeze rope attached to the bottom of the balloon from which the professor planned to jump formed a half-hitch knot around the neck of young Eddie. Redmond let go of the trapeze to avoid choking the youth further.

Eddie became entangled in the tether ropes on the strip of open ground east of the ferry landing and went soaring like a rocket, leaving his cap behind on the ground. The professor, dressed in spangled tights, did not make it aloft that fateful day. Women fainted, children cried and grown men averted their eyes.

The trapeze rope around his neck choked Eddie as he ascended. The lad reached above his head to take the strain off his thin neck. His arms began to tire as he sailed high over a southeast Portland lime kiln. To aid his aching arms, Eddie hauled himself up far enough to get the three-quarter-inch rope in his teeth. His teeth and arms worked in tandem, making his hold on life less painful. The ride was no lark.

Eddie looked down and saw the ground coming up to meet him. Seven minutes later, before the balloon collapsed in an adjacent field, he was dragged along the road to Milwaukie. When his feet hit solid ground, Eddie freed himself from the rope and started toward home.

"I was moving along on a pretty smart clip," Eddie remembered, "when I saw a horse and rider coming." It was Eddie's boyhood friend Willie Davey, who saw Eddie go aloft and followed him southward two miles from the ascension site at the east side of the ferry landing. Eddie's only complaints were that he suffered a chafed neck and a lost hat.

"I want to go home to mama and papa," Eddie told an *Oregonian* reporter arriving on the scene. "They will be uneasy about me, as I [was] suppose[d] to have stayed home this afternoon. Some of the boys were going to the balloon ascension and I could not resist the temptation of going with them. I am sorry I am not at home now."

When he was asked how he felt about the ride by a member of a crowd that had gathered, young Hall said, "Mighty funny. I thought I was a goner for a while, but I am still alive. I'll never monkey around anymore balloons; I have had enough of it. Where is my hat? I want to go home."

A derby passed among the crowd collected $5.87, which Eddie accepted. He remarked that it was the largest amount he ever possessed. A man gave Eddie a card from the Moore Photographic Parlor and asked him to come downtown. Dusk was approaching, and the Hall family cow needed milking before his parents left the Codray's theater to return to the family home on Powell Valley Road near today's Southeast 50th Avenue.

Eddie became a celebrity for a week and went downtown to have his picture taken. Moore hung up burlap and rope resembling the bottom of a balloon, posing Eddie standing on tiptoe and clinging desperately to a rope wrapped around his neck. The negative was cut below Eddie's feet to give the appearance that he was hanging in the air. The picture was displayed in a drugstore window on Southwest Front Street and sold for a dime.

One realtor mentioned that Eddie flew over the finest piece of ground during his flight—a new subdivision near Milwaukie Road and Southeast Holgate Street, where Eddie landed. Eddie told his story at an exhibition at the state fair in Salem and sold his picture for ten cents. Eddie never went aloft again.

Eddie Hall's story lived on for years. He gave a radio account of his 1889 adventure and published it in local newspapers. Even years later, he told his story during the Oregon centennial in 1959.

The first man in Oregon to jump from a balloon by parachute was witnessed by three thousand people on September 15, 1889. The balloon was cut loose at 6:10 p.m., and five minutes later, Professor Redmond jumped at three thousand feet, landing on a picket fence. Except for a bruised left hand, he escaped injury that day.

The balloon, relieved of the aeronaut's weight, shot into the air, ascending out of sight for fifteen minutes. It slowly landed three miles south of the launch site at the Jefferson Street Ferry landing. The only difficulty Redmond experienced was holding on to the parachute. Most aeronauts have loops into which they insert their hand before jumping, but for reasons unknown, the professor did not use them.

On November 10, 1889, Redmond descended from a parachute at two thousand feet and performed daring aerobatic feats in midair, such as hanging by the toes and swinging back and forth like a pendulum in view of three thousand spectators, who applauded loudly. The balloon, after rising to four thousand feet, turned upside down, collapsed and fell to the ground intact in southeast Portland.

The professor returned to Portland the next year, giving exhibitions along with Australian Bertha Onzola, the wife of balloonist Arthur Cosgrove. During one ascension on April 12, 1890, the pair rose five thousand feet, after which Redmond parachuted, leaving Bertha to pilot the balloon. At Centralia, Washington, Redmond landed in a tree and then fell seventy feet to the ground, stunned. This element of danger is part of what makes ascensions a thrilling attraction.

Professor Redmond lost his life near Snohomish, Washington, when his balloon fell three hundred feet into the pine woods on June 1, 1890. He was buried at Lone Fir Cemetery in Portland, Oregon. The *Oregonian* commented that "his death was the natural result of the folly that tempted it. It is the result of chance rather than skill that this result, was so long delayed since it was likely to occur."

Arthur Cosgrove went aloft six weeks later at East Portland, then a separate city from Portland, on August 10, 1890. He was despondent because of a love affair between his wife, Bertha, and Professor Redmond and went aloft intoxicated and without his strap and safety belt. Cosgrove's last words to those on the ground were, "I've known you all for a long time. You have all been good friends to me, but I will never see you alive again." He kissed his young son goodbye. Minutes later, he jumped to his death from a balloon, choosing to not open his parachute.

A.A. Kobe

A.A. Kobe of Wenatchee, Washington, was born in 1886. He performed twice at the Walla Walla fairgrounds. His first ascension came in 1910. He holds the record for balloon ascension preparation at six minutes from the time the fires started to heat the air until takeoff to the sky above.

To start the inflation, performers built a trench eighteen feet long and put barrels in the ground with steel pipes. Fires built inside the trench sent heated air into the balloons. The balloon remained in the air until it began to cool and then descended, but usually the balloon would stay aloft for at least ten minutes.

Kobe used three parachutes at a time to descend back to earth. His only accident took place in Ellensburg when a parachute split 1,800 feet above the ground. He came down on a hillside, resulting in a yearlong stay in a hospital. Over eighteen years, Kobe averaged five balloon ascensions per week for seven months of the year and about 125 parachute jumps per year.

CHAPTER 3

FAILED DREAMS AND HOAXES, 1895–1904

Rufus Porter

The first documented evidence of aviation in Oregon was a five-dollar stock certificate for the Aerial Navigation Company purchased by James H. Wilson, who arrived in Oregon during September 1853. Wilson bought the stock certificate, which was issued on April 29, 1852, in Porter County, Indiana. He carried it overland inside the family Bible to Linn County, settling at Union Point near Albany.

Rufus Porter devised a dirigible in 1820 and built a model in 1833. It was viewed at an airport for aerial navigation, and it was cigar-shaped and driven by a screw propeller. A larger one with a car for passengers was exhibited in New York and Washington, D.C., around 1840. Porter had plans for transcontinental passenger flight in a seven-hundred-foot-long hydrogen-filled balloon. A propeller powered by a ten-horsepower steam engine drove the craft forward, and fins at the rear controlled its direction. It would be able to transport 150 gold prospectors to California at $200 each at a speed of fifty to ninety miles per hour.

Porter stated in a postscript to his "Aeroport Prospectus" that "it is confidently believed that by this invention unexplored regions may be examined, and the light of civilization and Christianity may be disseminated through benighted lands with facility; and that the world will honor the names of those who now subscribe to the introduction of an invention calculated to confer immense benefits upon the entire human race."

Scientific American magazine, which Porter cofounded in 1845, stated that "the project is so grand and vast it is enough to make Mount Vesuvius burst out in fiery laughter."

H.V. Wiley, the commander of the giant dirigible USS *Macon*, said in 1935 that he was surprised "to find out many of the things incorporated in a modern airship had been forecast by Mr. Porter." This included the conception of dynamic control through rudder and elevators, the fact that the airship was safe from lightning and its viability as a means of transport like the Graf Zeppelins beginning in 1911.

CAPTAIN J.W. KERN

Captain John W. Kern, an Oregon pioneer of 1853 and steamboat captain living in Portland, planned an airship with a fantastic design. His one-thousand-foot-long fish-shaped airship would float in the air like a fish swimming in water.

The machine was to run on gasoline and be made of airtight aluminum containing hydrogen for lifting power. The first proposal for a lighter-than-air machine came in 1670, when Francisco de Lana realized that a sealed vacuum would weigh less than an equal volume of air. His proposed flying craft consisted of a basket suspended beneath four copper globes, each containing a vacuum.

Kern's design was similar to a proposed airship of Sir Hiram Maxim of England, having a three-quarter vacuum in an aluminum cylinder reinforced by strong interior ribs. The technological problems of constructing an aluminum container strong enough to contain hydrogen and withstand the atmospheric pressure on the outside made the design impossible to execute in 1895.

The unique feature of the Kern vessel are the paddle wheels, twenty-four feet in diameter, which raise the ship and propel it ahead, backward or downward. The wheels are attached to an axle shaft that runs through the ship at its center of gravity, and the wheels are completely controlled by the pilot. Although the wheels rotate in only two directions, the pilot can by manipulation of a lever connected with each bring the paddles into play at such points in the revolution as to cause them to exert their full power to lift or push forward or backward at the same time; also, one wheel can be made to move back while the other is pushing ahead. The pilot can give the vessel any course he desires.

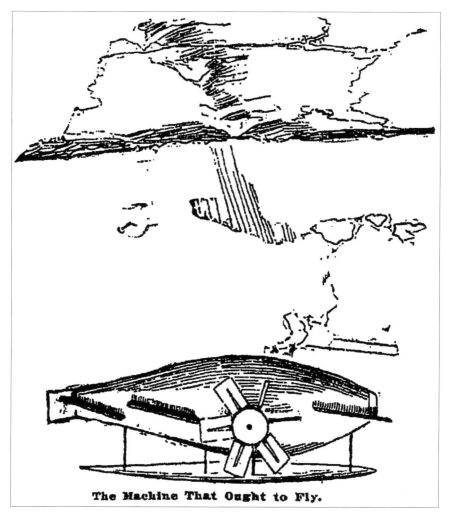

The Machine That Ought to Fly.

"Captain J.W. Kern Airship, 1896." *From the* Oregonian, *January 12, 1896.*

The propellers, designed in the shape of paddle wheels, are covered with feathers, make eighty-eight revolutions per minute and provide a lifting power of 4,320 pounds to raise the aircraft and power it.

Of course, Kern's airship never got off the ground, if a model of it was ever even built. Kern went on to invent and patent a range finder. He was inspired by a refrigeration process for manufacturing liquid air invented by Charles Tripler of New York. Captain Kern died on June 29, 1900, age sixty-two, in Philadelphia, Pennsylvania, while on a business trip marketing his range finder.

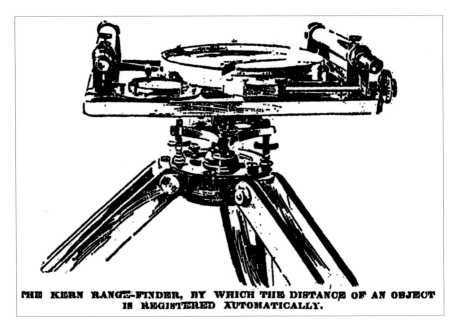

THE KERN RANGE-FINDER, BY WHICH THE DISTANCE OF AN OBJECT IS REGISTERED AUTOMATICALLY.

"Range Finder Invented by Captain Kern, 1899." *From the* Oregonian, *September 15, 1899.*

AIRSHIP HOAXES OF 1896

Books on airships like *A Dash to the Pole* by Herbert D. Ward influenced Oregonians' descriptions of airships and balloons. Jules Verne's stories about airships may also have influenced sky watchers in California and Oregon after his book *The Flying Clipper* was published in English in 1887, suggesting the possibility of an aluminum airship powered by electric motors.

France announced in 1893 that it would construct a large directional airship or dirigible. The rigid-frame airship of cigar shape was 203 feet in length and 43 feet at its greatest diameter; it flew at fourteen miles per hour. The next year, Germany planned to construct an airship, and the U.S. military also wanted a cigar-shaped airship of its own.

Mass sightings of airships across California began on November 19, 1896, as mysterious lights visible near Eureka and the next day near Tulare were thought to be either French, German or even American airships. In the evening, Sacramento residents reported a light "attached to some aircraft." In Oakland, witnesses spied an aircraft with huge fanlike propellers and giant wings attached to each side of the craft. During the evening of November 22, Sacramento residents watched a brilliant arc light travel to the southwest.

On November 24, 1896, local boys saw an airship over McMinnville, Oregon—or perhaps only some lights in the heavens. This was the first reported sightings seen in the nighttime sky of airships that originated in California.

The *Oregonian* reported "An Oakland Airship" on November 29, 1896. When a display of aerial lights caused by trolley cars lit up the sky on December 1, 1896, the newspaper reassured readers that it was not an airship, even though one man claimed that the searchlight of the famous California airship turned on Portland.

A vast majority of Oregon-based newspapers labeled the California stories a hoax to sell newspapers. The *Marshfield Coos Bay News* judged, "If it was a genuine flying machine, there would be for it to meander around the heavens at night." The *Portland Evening Telegram* wrote, "It is news to say that the ship has not been seen in Portland" and argued that it seems to have almost missed Oregon completely. Other Oregon newspapers called it "California's Fake" and "an entirely sensational piece of fiction" akin to sea serpent tales. One Oregon political writer observed that candidates for office are as "thick as airships in California."

The chief of the U.S. Weather Bureau, Wilis L. Moore, believed that the lights on airships seen all over the country were kites, and he was correct

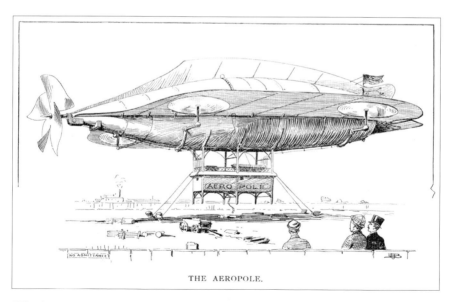

THE AEROPOLE.

"The Aeropole Dirigible." *From* A Dash to the Pole *by Herbert D. Ward (1892), author's copy.*

in one instance. Beginning in 1894, Ray Steel flew kites that could carry fifteen pounds and reached nine hundred feet in altitude at Long Beach, Washington; one was covered by yellow cloth, and another was a weather bureau kite. He also flew one kite carrying a Chinese lantern, reported as the planet Mars until the lantern went out.

These airship sightings were visions of steerable or directional balloons, spurred by a belief in technology where all things seemed helped foster the development of the dirigible airship comparable to the UFO sightings of 1947 and black aircraft of the present.

FUNNEL-SHAPED AIRCRAFT

Edward de Jongh of Portland proposed a wedge-shaped funnel air aircraft in 1896. The front edge of the flying wing was called a "supporting plane," which was as sharp as a knife and served as the main lifting surface according to Bernoulli's principle, whereby air flowing over a curved upper surface provides lift. The craft contained no lifting gas like hydrogen or helium.

The aircraft was driven by fan wheels powered by compressed air. A rudder controlled lateral movements after the craft became airborne. The type of engine was not specified in De Jongh's design.

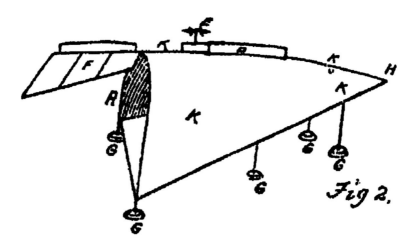

"Funnel Craft." By Edward de Jongh. *From the* Oregonian, *December 27, 1896.*

E.F. FABER

E.F. Faber of Portland drew up an airship design in 1900. The German-born Faber claimed to have worked with Count Zeppelin and needed $100,000 to construct the one-hundred-foot-long craft. The airship was a cigar-shaped dirigible made of aluminum, filled with hydrogen gas and steered by rudders at each end; it had great power and low weight.

Mr. Faber should have approached the War Department instead of Portland investors. He set up a string of loaded torpedoes that acted as a keel to stabilize the vessel in its proper position while aloft. The torpedoes were filled with gun cotton, nitroglycerin and dynamite. The airship could descend to attack enemy garrisons and battleships, as well as be used for observation. So much for the peaceful vision of aviation held by Octave Chanute.

THE DAWSON CITY

E.F. DeBorl, a Portland mechanic, formed the Portland to Dawson City Aerial Navigation Company in 1898 to construct an airship. Chambers of aluminum filled with gas would help lift the aircraft from the ground. The front of the craft has a knife-shaped edge to minimize air resistance. The ship was to be powered through the air by twenty-four-foot-diameter propellers with blades eight feet wide spinning at two hundred miles per hour.

The airship design used aluminum like Captain Kern's proposed airship. Titanium, discovered in 1791, would prove to be a much lighter and stronger metal, but it was not refined enough to use in manufacturing until 1940. The Soviets were the first to use titanium in aircraft parts in 1950.

The lack of motive power to turn propellers was another reason for the failure of these 1890s designs. Steam power proved impractical, although Samuel Langley constructed a twenty-five-pound steam-powered glider fueled by alcohol in 1896, but it never had the power to carry a man. The steam engine of 1900 was heavy and inefficient. And it was extremely dangerous when used beneath the highly flammable hydrogen balloon and dirigible. The development of the internal combustion engine by Nicolaus Otto in 1876 later made powered airships practical.

THE UNDER-POWERED KITE

Grant Keys worked as a firefighter on the Oregon Navigational Railroad. He erected a shed on Cricket Flat near Elgin during the summer of 1903, months before the Wright brothers' successful flight at Kitty Hawk, North Carolina, to build a heavier-than-air flying vehicle. He tried a powered flight in an aircraft of his own design on a hill above Morgan Lake three miles from La Grande. The glider was launched like a kite and rose one hundred feet in the air above Morgan Lake when pulled by six men. It was anchored to the earth with five hundred feet of rope and thoroughly evaluated before an independent flight attempt was made.

The steering gear consisted of two horizontal planes of canvas 3.1 by 10 feet placed in front of the aircraft. An observer described it as "made of wire, and bamboo, and used bicycle wheels for landing and had a basket strapped in place for the operator."

The trial trip of the 40-foot-long flying kite, constructed from 1,280 square feet of canvas and braced by wire and wood, was planned for July 1904. The propeller arms extended beneath the lower plane of the craft. Keys's aircraft weighed 550 pounds and failed to ascend with a fifteen-horsepower gasoline engine, which gave only 37 pounds of lift per horsepower.

Using a twenty-five-horsepower four-cylinder motor like that of the Pfitzner monoplane of 1909 would give twenty-three pounds of lift per horsepower. The main reason for Keys's failure, like with every heavier-than-aircraft of its era, was that the engine, weighing under one hundred pounds, proved too heavy and lacked the required power.

In comparison, the Pfitzner monoplane Curtiss engine drove two blade wooden propellers six feet in diameter at 1200rpm. The total weight was 508 pounds, and at 24 pounds lift per horsepower and 3.2 pounds carried per square foot of surface, the ratio was 5.17 to 1.

Keys traveled to Portland on November 13, 1904, after being requested to bring his airplane by the board of commissioners of the Lewis and Clark World Fair of 1905. Instead, Keys gave up his airplane experiments, traveling to work as a dredge engineer on the Panama Canal. In April 1906, he returned to the United States and moved to Illinois and later Detroit, Michigan.

Meanwhile, in August 1906, Alexander Graham Bell abandoned the box kite in favor of a tetrahedral kite because the support used in the box kite hindered lift. Bell contended correctly that the lack of a light motor having sufficient power was the only obstacle remaining in the way of constructing a successful flying machine.

The French aviator Louis Bleriot, who was the first to fly across the English Channel, began experimenting with airplanes in 1906. The third of Bleriot's designs was a machine with elliptical cells that was launched on floats in the Seine River to haul it up like a kite. Maybe Keys's kite launch and design were not so far-fetched, after all. However, Bleriot abandoned the elliptical design because of lack of stability and then constructed his "Number 4," which was a box kite.

CHAPTER 4

DIRIGIBLES, 1905–1910

Thomas Baldwin

Inventors and engineers tried for seven decades to propel elongated cigar-shaped balloons with a car underneath and a screw propeller, all of which failed. Around 1902, Thomas Scott Baldwin of San Francisco constructed the *California Eagle*, with a paddle wheel, based on outdated marine technology. The *Eagle* was powered by a Dion-Bouton engine. He failed to control his balloon on April 23, 1904, due to engine trouble.

Baldwin also constructed the *Big Glory*, the largest balloon constructed to date, containing 140,000 cubic feet of hydrogen gas. The balloon was launched from Denver, Colorado, on August 31, 1904. It was planned for the balloon to reach New York if possible.

He perfected the rigid airship or dirigible later that year; it was powered by a seven-horsepower Hercules motorcycle engine made by Glen H. Curtiss. Hydrogen gas, made in a tank located outside the balloon shed, was pumped into the bag. The materials necessary to produce hydrogen gas are sulfuric acid, calcium chloride and iron fillings. The hydrogen is purified by passing the gas through lime and caustic soda. The gas is then transmitted to the airship through a large rubber hose.

The hydrogen-filled dirigible the *California Arrow* was flown twice at the St. Louis World Fair of 1904. Baldwin also built three dirigibles for the Portland Exposition of 1905: the *Angelus*, the *City of Portland* and a reproduction of the *Arrow*. These two rigid framed airships consisted of a bulging gas bag, a sputtering gas engine, a simple rudder and a plank platform. The direction of the ship was mostly controlled by the pilot's position on the plank.

Baldwin, known as the "Father of the American Dirigible," commented on his 1905 dirigible flights at Portland, Oregon: "We have shown the air can be successfully navigated and that is all. Whenever it is, it will come in a snap like the telegraph, telephone, electric lights, and other great inventions. The real solution will be something that else that will be able to hold its own to the elements."

Baldwin went on to race balloons from Denver, Colorado, during 1902, but heavier-than-air craft proved to be the solution Baldwin sought. The Wright brothers' flights at Kitty Hawk during 1903 proved the answer. The air shows of January 11–13, 1910, at Los Angeles and Portland showed the future of controlled flight in this country and airshows.

Lincoln Beachey and Roy Knabenshue ascended in two small dirigibles and maneuvered their airships, but as the *Oregonian* reported, it was "nothing to thrill the spectators." On June 14, 1910, Beachey entered a monoplane at the Indianapolis, Indiana Air Show.

*A*NGELUS

The first controlled flight in the Pacific Northwest came courtesy of the dirigible *Angelus* over the Lewis and Clark Exposition grounds at Guild's Lake, heading to a Willamette River dock at Oaks Park on July 18, 1905. The north winds were too strong for the dirigible to return to the exposition site. When the engine is started on a dirigible, the propeller is set in motion. The *Angelus*'s eight-foot-by-three-foot-long propeller blades were powered by a seven-horsepower one-cylinder engine. It does not make any difference whether the wind velocity is eight miles per hour or zero. The *Angelus*'s propellers exerted a force of eight miles per hour in still air, and that is its total resistance against any wind. Any wind above eight miles per hour would stall the dirigible.

The *Angelus* was sixty-five feet long, forty feet wide, contained eighteen thousand cubic feet of hydrogen gas and weighed five hundred pounds total with the aeronaut. Lincoln Beachey, who piloted the airship, was born in San Francisco on March 3, 1887. Beachey made his first flight in a dirigible that was owned by George F. Heaton at Oakland, California, during February 1905.

"Airship City of Portland, Nosing Out of Hangar at Lewis and Clark Exposition, 1905." *Oregon Historical Society, folder 598, no. 47383.*

"Airship Angelus at Lewis and Clark Exposition, 1905." *Oregon Historical Society, folder 598, no. 202.*

Beachey took his place under the gas bag of the *Angelus* by standing on a steel bar alongside the keel. He ascended to five hundred feet by moving away from the gasoline motor at the center of the keel toward the stern; then he continued to one thousand feet, seeking favorable winds. When Beachey wanted to descend, he walked ahead of the engine to the front of the catwalk.

For two hours, the *Angelus* hovered over Portland like a great bird, moving slowly southward across the sky, appearing in control; nonetheless, it battled an eight-mile-per-hour wind from the north. Beachey commented that with calmer air currents, he could have made it as steerable by its six-foot-by-ten-foot-long rudder as a sailboat.

The *Angelus* ascended to one thousand feet on August 3, 1905, landing in St. Johns, and on two other days, the airship failed to return to the shed at the exposition grounds because of engine failure. Baldwin gave up on the *Angelus* and brought his *California Arrow II* to Portland for the planned air races. The second *Arrow* never flew and was replaced by a new dirigible, the *City of Portland*, which was constructed at the 1905 world's fair grounds.

Aeronautics Day at Portland's world fair was held on August 12, 1905. Baldwin's dirigible *Angelus* and the *Knox Gelatine*, owned by George Tomlinson of Syracuse, New York, were scheduled to be sent aloft in an airship race. Baldwin decided to fall back on the *Arrow* design and construct a new airship when the *Angelus* failed to make headway against a moderate breeze.

Guild's Lake overlook, 2024. Site of 1905 World's Fair, where dirigibles ascended. *Photo by Murray N. Stone.*

"Balloon Exposition, Portland, Circa 1905." *Oregon Historical Society, folder 1059, no. 11008.*

Baldwin's new airship, the *City of Portland*, was built on the exposition grounds at half the size of the *Angelus*. Beachey piloted the dirigible on its trial flight on August 19, 1905, in a flight lasting twenty minutes. The *City of Portland* was half the size of the old *Angelus*, proved more navigable by cruising against a six-mile-per-hour north wind and, more importantly, was able to land within twenty feet of its starting point, a world first. Beachey piloted six additional flights, all viewed as successful because the dirigible returned to its starting point.

The gas bag of *City of Portland* was torn on September 2, 1905, when the airship collided with a tree on the east side of the Willamette River. The gas bag of the *Gelatine* was used for further flights by Beachey and on the record flight of September 15, 1905. This flight went from the fairgrounds to the Jackson Tower at Southwest Fifth Avenue and Southwest Yamhill and returned to the Aeronautic Concourse. The *Oregon Journal* wrote that the airship "sailed as gracefully as [a] sea pigeon" over Portland. The fifty-minute, five-mile flight at fifteen miles per hour broke the world's speed record for aerial navigation.

On September 19, 1905, Beachey delivered the first message ever delivered by dirigible to General Constant Williams at the Fort Vancouver barracks. The letter was written by Theodore Hardee, assistant to the exposition president. The gasoline ran out as Beachey was returning from Vancouver against the wind and forced a landing on the east bank of the Willamette River. General Williams replied, "Captain Baldwin is to be congratulated on the success of his dirigible airship and his choice of a pilot."

Beachey made two circling flights around the exposition grounds on September 22, 1905. Four days later, on September 26, 1905, Beachey took off, flying to three hundred feet in elevation from the fairgrounds southeast to the roof of the Chamber of Commerce Building at Southwest Stark and Southwest Fourth Avenues. Willing hands pulled the eight-thousand-cubic-foot *City of Portland* airship down to the roof, where Beachey delivered the first messages carried by a dirigible, making the first recorded landing on a building. Beachey then circled around the Jackson Tower and turned west to Southeast Twenty-Third Avenue, traveling at fifteen miles per hour and arriving thirty-three minutes later at the starting point. It was a record-breaking controlled flight of an airship from the fair site at Guild's Lake to the heart of Portland and back.

The last two flights of the Portland Exposition of 1905 piloted by Beachey came on September 30, 1905. The flights, one in the morning and one in the afternoon, lasted twenty minutes each. The planned flight to Vancouver and back was canceled because of the weather. "I am well satisfied with the

"Knox-Gelatin, Airship at 1905 Portland Lewis and Clark Exposition (World' Fair)." *Oregon Historical Society, folder 1059, Aviation, no. 50697.*

summer's work," said Baldwin. "I think some progress has been made and I am going to keep right on going."

Baldwin and Beachey departed Portland for Los Angeles on October 20, 1905, where two new motors, a two-cylinder and a four-cylinder model, were available for future flight experiments. In 1906 in Cleveland, Ohio, Beachey had an airship collapse under him, rendering him unconscious. The next year, he flew over New York City and landed in the water. Beachey and Roy Knabenshue tried to race at the Los Angeles Aviation Exposition on January 17, 1910, but gave up after half a mile when winds pushed them back to the starting point. The next day, Beachey ascended alone.

Captain Baldwin designed a U.S. Army Signal Corps dirigible in 1908 and flew it at the Indianapolis balloon races for endurance and distance during June 1909. Later, he designed his own airplane, the *Red Devil*, and made the first airplane trip across the Mississippi River.

Lincoln Beachey gave up dirigibles and constructed a monoplane during January 1911; he was the first aviator to fly around the U.S. Capitol building and over Niagara Falls. He was killed on March 15, 1915, in San Francisco when his monoplane went into an uncontrolled dive in excess of two hundred miles per hour one mile above the Panama-Pacific Exposition. The wings buckled, and the plane and Beachey sank out of sight into San Francisco Bay.

CHAPTER 5

THE AVIATORS, 1910–1924

CHARLES K. HAMILTON:
THE FIRST FLYER IN OREGON

E. Henry Wemme, described by the *Oregonian* as a "capitalist" and head of the Automobile Club, organized an aeronautic club in Portland, Oregon, during November 1909, offering $150,000 to bring an aviation meet to Portland. He wanted to own the first plane in Oregon and sought to buy a French-built monoplane from Louis Bleriot, who had sold more than 140 of the model No. XI, which Bleriot flew across the English Channel.

Bleriot wanted $80,000 to come to Los Angeles for a week of flights, and Hubert Latham quoted $35,000. Wemme passed on the two French aviators' prices to the California City of Angels and was unwilling to wait any longer to buy a Bleriot monoplane.

Wemme was in a hurry because he had already been eclipsed by Colonel Frank H. Johnson of San Francisco, who bought the first automobile on the West Coast before Wemme bought one in 1899. The colonel had just purchased the first plane, a Curtiss model. Wemme also purchased a Curtiss biplane for $5,000 that Charles K. Hamilton, a member of the Glenn H. Curtiss organization, flew at the Los Angeles Airshow on January 16–17, 1910; the first International Aviation Exhibition where Hamilton also flew was held in the United States, running for ten days beginning January 10, 1910. The next air show was held at San Diego, California, on January 25,

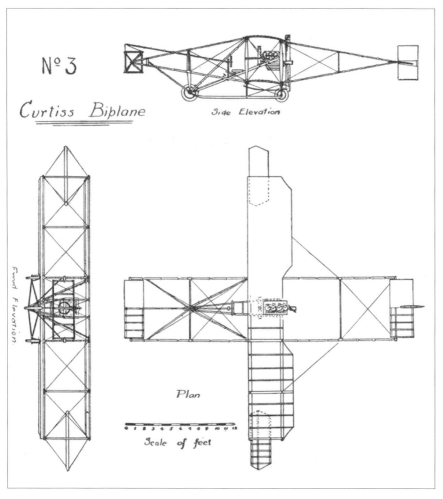

"Curtiss Biplane, No. 3." Illustration by Grover Loening. *From* Scientific American, *supplement, October 22, 1910, reprinted 2006.*

1910, where Hamilton used the same biplane that Glenn Curtiss flew at Reims, France, winning the speed prize on August 29, 1909.

The Curtiss machines in Los Angeles won prizes for speed, quick starts and perfect starts—"a light quick machine" in which Glenn Curtiss broke the speed record. The Farman biplane, flown by French aviator Louis Paulhan, was a heavier, slower craft, breaking records for altitude of 4,135 feet and cross-country distance record of 47.5 miles while carrying two passengers.

The Farman racing plane weighed 1,050 pounds and had a surface of 350 square feet and the wing spread of 28 feet; 21 pounds are lifted per

"Curtiss Style Plane Assembled at Salem, OR." *Oregon Historical Society, folder 1059.*

horsepower, with 3 pounds per square foot of surface. The aspect ratio of swing spread to wing width is 4.2 to 1.

An airplane flight from Portland to Mount Hood was announced by Hamilton on February 25, 1910, to Oregon newspapers. Hamilton hoped to establish new altitude and cross-country distance records in a Curtiss biplane. "I will obtain the effect of my life to reach Mt. Hood," Hamilton wrote in a telegram from Douglas, Arizona. Hamilton's planned flight around Mount Hood on March 7, 1910, would reach seven thousand feet and cover 106 miles, but it never took place despite a $1,000 reward by the Portland Aeronautic Club to beat Paulhan's cross-country distance record.

This Curtiss biplane of double-bowed shape weighed 550 pounds and had a four-cylinder, twenty-five-horsepower Curtiss motor that provided 22 pounds of lift per horsepower and 2.5 pounds per square foot of surface. The motor placed at the rear drives directed a two-bladed wooden propeller at 1200rpm. The propeller had a pitch of five feet and a diameter of six feet. The maximum speed was forty-seven miles per hour. The aspect ratio was 5.65 to 1.

A fifteen-square-foot keel placed in the rear steadied the craft. The mounting was on three rubber-tired wheels rigidly fixed to the ash and birch frame, along with the larger outriggers of bamboo, with no springs provided. Small cables as well as wires were used for bracing.

The Curtiss plane, purchased by Wemme, was transported by train and assembled by local inventor Walter E. Donelly for a display at the 1910 Portland Auto Show. Wemme was the first man in Oregon to own an automobile, which he bought in 1898. Now he owned the first plane in the state, and he telegraphed from Hot Springs, Arkansas, his desire that Hamilton be the pilot.

Hamilton was five feet, seven inches tall, weighed 125 pounds, had large ears like monoplanes, blue eyes and red hair. He transported the first Curtiss biplanes to Oregon from Los Angeles by train.

The larger Curtiss model weighed 1,150 pounds; 22.6 pounds were carried per horsepower, and 3.64 pounds were carried per foot of surface. A fifty-horsepower, eight-cylinder engine drove a 7-foot propeller at 1100rpm. The supporting planes had a spread of 32 feet, a depth of 5 feet and an area of 316 square feet. The aspect ratio was 6.4 to 1. The elevation rudder was 31 square feet and the directional rudder 7.5 square feet in area. The rear horizontal keel had an area of 17.5 square feet, while the ailerons were each 27 square feet in size.

Hamilton arrived in Portland on March 5, 1910, wearing a gray hat, a suit and a double-breasted short leather coat, smoking a Turkish cigarette as he strolled around inspecting the Curtiss aircraft. He then sat in the pilot seat in front of the engine.

Hamilton rocked back and forth to evaluate the two balancing planes five feet apart, which were made of one layer of Baldwin rubber silk tacked to spruce ribs and laced to the frame. Then Hamilton grabbed the steering wheel, which was attached to a long bamboo rod, and pulled it back and forth to evaluate the altitude rudder mounted at the front of the plane on bamboo outriggers. Turning the steering wheel, which was connected by cables, Hamilton observed the left and right swing of the direction rudder at the rear of the craft. Shifting the pilot's seat left preserves the lateral balance by means of a brace to the balancing planes located midway between each of the wing tips.

The gas engine was cranked, the magneto responded and the whirl of the thin, durable propeller was heard between the chugs of the unmuffled engine. Two burly men held the plane down as it quivered. The plane proceeded down the grounds of the Portland Livestock Association, now the Rose City Golf Course, at twenty-five miles per hour. The frail plane skimmed the ground when the wheels stopped turning.

Overlook of Rose City Golf Course, looking south—Mount Tabor is in the background. Here Oregon's first airplane took off, piloted by Charles Hamilton, March 1910. *Photo by Murray N. Stone.*

The plane looked like a gigantic insect, its long, thin bamboo limbs stretching. Then it was a foot off the ground. Suddenly there was a slight depression in the ground, and the plane went down for a second and then sprang upward. Then ten thousand spectators suddenly saw the plane dipping downward and then rising again in a 500-foot-high parabola curve. Hamilton turned off the engine and glided to a perfect landing, cruising on the ground 150 feet by its own momentum.

This five-minute flight by Hamilton was the first airplane flight in Oregon. Hamilton also won a race by one lap with a Buick automobile; driving around the five-eighths-mile-long course was not spectacular, although the spectators were able to watch the first flight taking place in the Pacific Northwest.

Hamilton made another short flight the next day with Wemme's plane, but it came down after flying one hundred yards. Hamilton claimed that the propeller was not properly adjusted, and he did not want to advertise the plane.

Portland pilot Walter E. Donnelly was practicing with Wemme's biplane later that day, cruising eastward a foot above the ground before a crowd of five thousand spectators, who crowded in too closely the day after Hamilton's first flight. While the plane cruised by on the track, it veered several feet before knocking one man down. Then Donnelly struck the horse

"Automobile Races!" ad. *From the* Oregonian, *July 7, 1912.*

of a mounted police officer, knocking both to the ground; he injured four others before he could stop the engines. Donnelly was ultimately thrown from his seat, uninjured, but the plane was turned on its side, sustaining damage that was easily repaired.

On the final day of the Portland air show, March 7, 1910, Hamilton made his longest glide to date, lasting eight minutes from height of one thousand feet. Afterward, he made a flight of two miles flying around and over Rocky Butte. It was not the planned trip around Mount Hood that he promised during late February. The "Hamilton Glide" he invented consisted of stopping the engine while five hundred feet in the air and gliding down in a controlled descent mimicking the birds, and he would repeat the glide at exhibition sites.

Hamilton traveled on to Seattle and was almost killed there on March 13, 1910. He went on to fly successfully at Tacoma, March 19–22, 1910, making three flights where "from start to finish [he] had the biplane under control," according to the *Oregonian.*

He later suffered two crashes during 1910, one at Sacramento and the other at Memphis, and other near misses the next year. In a thirty-three-minute flight between Sacramento and Marysville, California, on March 15, 1912, Hamilton achieved a new American speed record of 78.9 miles per hour.

In his four-and-a-half-year career, Hamilton broke his collarbone twice, fractured two ribs, dislocated his left arm, fractured his right knee and dislocated both legs. He almost died in a balloon crash in 1906 and again in a Ludlow airplane in 1908. Hamilton died of pneumonia at the age of twenty-three in New York on January 23, 1914, which is quite remarkable compared to the more than one hundred pilots who died in airplane crashes before him.

JOHN C. BURKHART: THE HOMEBORN AVIATOR

John Connor Burkhart, a mechanic born in Albany, Oregon, built the first airplane to fly in the state during early 1910. Burkhart's first love was photography; he enjoyed taking pictures of seagulls in flight, hoping to discover the secrets of flight like the brothers Otto and Gustave Lilienthal at the Baltic seashore.

Orville Wright wrote on May 13, 1908, that "J.C. Burkhart of Ithaca, New York, disguised as a native was present," viewing their test flights at Paris. He was present when Glen N. Curtiss won the Scientific American Cup on July 4, 1908, at Hammondsport, New York.

Burkhart went to Cornell to study mechanical engineering. He learned to fly along with Oscar Trolicht at Hammondsport, New York. Their plane, piloted by Burkhart on September 2, 1908, flew three miles in five minutes at Cornell University, launched from a wooden monorail copied from the Wrights' system.

Burkhart believed in aviation's future, telling a reporter, "I am confident that before long aeroplanes carrying 20 passengers and capable of traveling at the rate of 100 mph will not be uncommon." His second biplane was displayed uncompleted at the Portland automobile show, located inside the Oregon Armory, which ran January 21–29, 1910, one day after the International Air Exposition ended at Los Angeles.

The first airplane Burkhart built in Albany crashed from a height of thirty feet into a pasture fence on March 10, 1910. The plane took off from a monorail, powered by a forty-horsepower, eight-cylinder, air-cooled engine, weighing 150 pounds, that was designed by Curtiss. The engine was supported between the planes immediately behind the aviator's seat; the biplane weighed 460 pounds in total and had a wingspan of thirty-four feet.

An unusual feature about this plane was its method of lateral control and transverse control to make smooth turns. To bank the aircraft, the flimsy wings were bent or warped by means of levers and strips near the pilot's shoulders, as invented by the Wright brothers. In Burkhart's unique system, the wings were fixed so it could make smooth turns via lengthening the wings of one side of the plane while shortening the other. At one point, Burkhart lost control due to the failure of the craft's unique "double rudder" steering system of artificial inclination, but he escaped uninjured.

Burkhart's second flight was not spectacular, but his airplane did lift from its skids and fly two hundred yards on April 9, 1910, at Albany, Oregon. Despite another crash, it qualified as the first successful flight by an Oregonian in Oregon. He sold the plane for twelve dollars to a Dufur, Oregon resident.

The next plane built by Burkhart and William Crawford, with its perfected "double rudder," made exhibition flights around Portland and north to the Vancouver, Washington Army Barracks during September 1912. His third designed plane was a biplane with a hydroplane attachment for aquatic takeoffs and landings. The highest flight reached an altitude of 1,500 feet over Portland and lasted for twelve minutes on April 24, 1913.

Burkhart married Mabel C. Goss of Albany on June 1, 1913, promising to give up flying, and hired Louis T. Barin, a Portland druggist, to take his place. Ms. Burkhart's fears of crashes were real because so many flyers had crashed and died. Eugene Ely, a Portland automobile mechanic and aviator, died in Macon, Georgia, becoming the fiftieth aviator fatality in 1911. When asked how long he expected to remain in the flying business, Ely replied during August to Henry Wemme, just two months before his fatal crash on October 19, 1911, "Oh, I'll do like the rest of them[,] keep it up until I am killed."

Burkhart's third plane made three flights during 1914 from the aero dome located at Northeast Fifteenth and Northeast Everett Streets. Burkhart sold the plane to his prodigy Louis T. Barin, who made a twelve-minute, fifty-mile-per-hour flight that attained an altitude of eight hundred feet. This new aircraft, built along with W.C. Crawford, was powered by a sixty-horsepower Roberts two-cycle engine. The pair manufactured the plane at the O.K. Jeffery Company in Portland.

The O.K. Jeffery Company, headed by Oliver King Jeffery, the president of the Oregon Homebuilders Association, became the main Portland manufacturer of spruce parts used in airplane construction; well-seasoned spruce was resilient and robust, an integral material to airplane construction before 1920. The local spruce supply was one of the main reasons, besides access to capital, that the Boeing Company began in Seattle, Washington.

The spruce parts for construction of speedy flyers were made inside a brick factory located at Northeast Thirty-Third Avenue and Northeast Broadway in Portland. Employing sixteen workers, the company finished wooden struts, beams and braces, shaped to form in Portland and shipped east. One thousand square feet of spruce were used for the construction of one airplane. The Jeffery plant could work twenty-five thousand square feet per day.

Burkhart next designed a pontoon hydroplane, piloted by J.H. Skening, which had a 125-horsepower Roberts engine, a forty-foot wingspan, with six feet between the two wings, and an eight-foot propeller. The hydroplane could climb nine hundred feet per minute at eighty-seven miles per hour when the Roberts engine revved up to its maximum of 1500rpm. Later, two flying boats were constructed of mahogany just for the private use of Skening and Jeffery.

Burkhart remained as engineer and designer for Jeffery and visited the Curtiss plant at Buffalo, New York, while his former student Louis Barin enlisted in the navy on February 5, 1917, as an instructor at Pensacola, Florida. The Aviation Section of the U.S. Signal Corps had only thirty-five officers capable of active duty as aviators and less than one thousand soldiers. There were fifty-five planes—fifty-one were outdated.

In July 1917, $640 million was appropriated by Congress for the expansion of the air service. Burkhart enlisted in the Army Air Corps during September 1917 as a captain, serving in the information and technical sections of the department of military aeronautics, and he was involved in the procurement of 8,075 training planes and 12,400 service planes within a year.

After the armistice, Captain Burkhart returned to Portland and his first love, photography. He worked as a portrait photographer and had exhibitions at the Portland Art Museum until tuberculosis forced him to give up his business and studio at the Worcester Building.

At the start of the 1920s, it was believed that long-distance flights were more important for aviation's future than exhibition stunts over large cities. Louis Barin served as a navigator aboard the Navy/Curtiss flying boat *NC-1* in its attempt to cross the Atlantic by way of the Azores during May 1919. However, only one plane, *NC-4*, flew on to Lisbon, Portugal. Nineteen days later, two British aviators made the first nonstop flight across the Atlantic in less than sixteen hours.

Ensign Barin died in an airplane collision on June 13, 1920, in San Diego, destroying all Burkhart's desire to work in the aviation field. Burkhart rode a motorcycle to Santa Barbara, California, in 1921, and continued his photography profession after a year's rest. His wife arranged exhibitions for his work in Portland and California after his death on May 13, 1926, at the age of forty-three.

Burkhart was the second man to fly in Oregon, one week after Charles Hamilton, and the second man, after Henry Wemme, to own a plane, but the public forgets second place. His partner, William Crawford, wrote a letter in 1931 to the *Oregonian* to extol Burkhart's achievements, and a full story was published in 1947 positioning him as "Oregon's First Plane Builder." He is currently not an inductee to the Oregon Aviation Hall of Fame.

In President Herbert Hoover's radio address of May 23, 1931, Burkhart was incorrectly mentioned at the Cornell University War Memorial as dying during World War I. Burkhart became a forgotten man, avoiding fame and recognition by abandoning flying in 1913 because of his wife's concerns and by moving to California to continue his career in photography.

SILAS CHRISTOFFERSON: STUNTMAN EXTRAORDINAIRE

Silas Christofferson was born near Des Moines, Iowa, in 1890 and moved with his family six years later. He attempted to fly in 1908 in a plane he constructed at Hidden's Pasture near Vancouver, Washington. He moved to Portland, Oregon, in 1910, working as a mechanic for the Fred A. Bennett Motor Company at Southwest Fifteenth Avenue and Southwest Alder Street; on Sundays, Silas raced cars at the Rose City Racetrack, now the Rose City Golf Course.

The Bennett-Christofferson Air Ship Company was incorporated at Salem on May 3, 1910. Christofferson and his brother Harry hunted geese from his plane in Coos County. They set a new world record when Harry shot twenty-seven geese during one flight. Next the brothers flew to Portland to prepare for a deer hunt. Soon after, a new Oregon law was passed prohibiting all hunting from an airplane.

During April 1911, Christofferson and his brother worked on their homebuilt monoplane, based on a later Bleriot design that had incorrect power specifications from a New York publisher. Their workshop was a tent at Northeast Dekum and Northeast Twenty-Eight Avenue in Portland, Oregon, where several flights of up to three hundred yards took place in a field across from the tent.

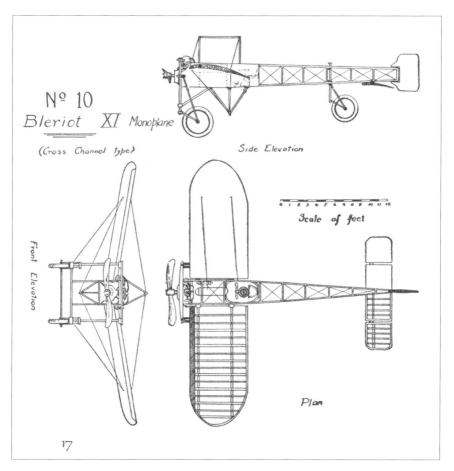

"Bleriot No. 10 Monoplane." *From* Scientific American, *supplement, October 22, 1910, reprinted 2006.*

Silas built a forty-horsepower gasoline engine weighing 250 pounds. The wingspan was forty feet, and the craft weighed 800 pounds in total. Due to the roughness of the ground, the propeller was damaged. The brothers moved to a smoother field at the artillery grounds at Fort Vancouver, Washington, during May 1911.

The Christofferson brothers re-evaluated the Bleriot design on June 13, 1911, at Fort Vancouver. They were not allowed to use the drill grounds in the morning and evening, when the army mules were turned out to graze and run.

Christofferson built a Bleriot-designed plane that had a 30-foot wingspan, a depth of 28.2 feet and surface area of 151 square feet, weighing a total of 650 pounds. The plane was braced above and below by wires from the central frame. To preserve the longitudinal stability, a fixed 17-square-foot horizontal keel was placed at the rear. The seat was in the back of the main frame.

A correctly designed Bleriot Model XI, with a twenty-three-horsepower three-cylinder Anziani motor, flew at thirty-six miles per hour on July 25, 1909, from Calais, France, to Dover, England. The motor drove a wooden propeller, two-bladed, 6.9 feet in diameter, at 1350rpm. Twenty-nine pounds were lifted per horsepower, and four and a half pounds were carried per foot of surface. The aspect ratio is 4.35 to 1.

An exhibition by Hubert Latham in California prompted Christofferson to take flying lessons in a high-powered Curtiss biplane during the spring of 1912. He left behind his underpowered plane at Vancouver, as it was unable to fly across the Columbia River because it required a fifty-horsepower motor due to changes to the elevation rudder, which was attached to a tapered keel much larger than in the original design.

Usually in the Curtiss plane school instructions, the beginner is given a twenty-five-horsepower plane by the instructor so the novice cannot ascend beyond a safe altitude. Due to the high power of the fifty-horsepower Rheims motor, Christofferson rose too high in the air and lost control of the plane, which crashed to the ground, causing multiple bruises to the pilot and destruction of the plane. Afterward, Christofferson returned to the Pacific Northwest on May 20, 1912, making daily flights over Vancouver.

He carried his future wife, Edna Beeker, as a passenger on his flights beginning on May 23, 1912; she sat on the wing. After the wedding, they flew in a pontoon-rigged Curtiss biplane in November, taking off from the Willamette River. Mrs. Christofferson held on to a bamboo strut, shrouded in a rubber overcoat, while Christofferson circled Portland, following the river south at seventy miles per hour to Oregon City, with his cap turned backward and without goggles during the one-hour flight.

He made the first crossing of the Columbia River from Vancouver to the Country Club Track on the north side of Southeast Stark Street, twelve miles east of Portland, on June 6, 1912, covering eight miles in eight minutes. Later, the plane was transported to downtown Portland to the roof of the Multnomah Hotel for his ultimate stunt.

This daredevil event took place during the Rose Festival on June 11, 1912, advertised as the "first flight from roof of building in aeroplane history." Christofferson poured gasoline into the sixty-horsepower engine, assisted by his brother Harry, for the Curtiss "Pusher style" plane on the roof of the

AEROPLANE FLIGHT

Silas Christofferson Will Fly From Roof of Multnomah Hotel, Tuesday, 2 P. M.

First flight from roof of building in aeroplane history. A limited number of admissions to roof will be sold. Tickets on sale Monday at Hotel Office

From the Oregonian, *June 8, 1912.*

ten-story hotel; a handcrafted ramp was made of overlapping fir boards, 20 feet wide and 150 feet long. Soon he was flying over the streets of Portland. Twelve minutes later, Christofferson landed at the Fort Vancouver parade grounds, carrying letters, making this the first interstate airmail delivery in the Pacific Northwest.

Christofferson explained the purpose of the flight to a reporter: "This is an age to do it first. Be original; do not copy. When a feat has been performed once the people tire of it and expect the next performer to give something new. That is the only reason I decided to make a flight from the top of the Multnomah Hotel."

Christofferson made four unsuccessful attempts at flying at Tillamook on July 4, 1912. Cross currents of wind from the bay proved too much for him to gain altitude. The aircraft was caught forty feet above the ground and, just as the pilot was about to raise the plane, dove down, crashing to the ground on its side. He returned to Vancouver the next day to fly around the military post.

Fred A. Bennet and Christofferson equipped their Curtiss biplane with a sixteen-foot-long pontoon and two floats below the lower wing tips to convert

"Curtiss Hydroplane After Accident at Astoria, OR." *Oregon Historical Society, folder 159, no. 57.*

it to a hydroplane. Walter Edwards set a hydroplane altitude record of two thousand feet on August 4, 1912, taking off from the Willamette River at the foot of Southwest Seventeenth Avenue and flying over Portland Harbor. They planned to use the hydroplane to deliver mail by air from Portland to Oregon City. The hydroplane was wrecked by a novice pilot who struck some driftwood.

The Curtiss biplane was converted back to a land plane. Walter Edwards (aka Walter Edward Kittel) used it to fly from the Waverly Country Club in Southeast Portland to Vancouver, carrying 1,500 pieces of mail weighing twenty-five pounds on August 12, 1912, after Edwards was sworn in as a mail carrier. "Don't make a botch of it, now, if I fail get the best doctor in the city," Edwards said to his assistants and the crowd before taking off from Portland, succeeding in making the first official interstate delivery of mail by airplane. Regular service to Vancouver was never planned by the U.S. Postal Service.

On his return flight back to the Oregon side of the Columbia River, Edwards quipped that "no dog will trouble me. He'd have to be a combination of a Russian Stag Hound and a seagull."

The interstate flights lasted only two days, proving little more than a stunt for the Aviation Exhibition sponsored by the Bennett Aero Company, which charged fifty cents to view the events, but they were a first. The letters were stamped: "US Aeromail Service. This letter was carried from Portland August 12, 1912, to Vancouver Wash. by Aviator Walter Edwards."

The chief inspector of the customs for the Portland Harbor saw a hydroplane at dusk during early September 1912 and became upset. The plane, which the inspector viewed as a motor-driven boat, had no lights, life preservers, bucket of sand, foghorn, bells or anchor and was therefore covered by federal maritime statutes, which allowed him to halt any hydroplane mail delivery from Portland to Oregon City.

Edwards and Christofferson departed company after the hydroplane flights were discontinued. Edwards purchased a plane from Claude Berlin that he wrecked in Centralia, Washington, on January 26, 1913, and went on to Ottawa, Canada, piloting Captain Thomas S. Baldwin's *Red Devil* airplane.

The fabulous Multnomah Hotel flight of June 11, 1912, was destined to be repeated, unlike the first mail flight of August 12, which was prevented by U.S. Post Office regulations. The components of the 1947 replica Curtiss biplane were lifted to the top of the Multnomah Hotel on September 17, 1995, where the parts were assembled, and the plane was "pushed down a runway off the roof."

The pilot, Tom Murphy, made the flight across the Columbia River to Vancouver in twelve minutes. A reproduction of this "Pusher style" aircraft has the engine and propeller mounted behind the pilot and is displayed at the Pearson Air Museum in Vancouver, Washington, along with a video documentary of the re-creation of the historic flight.

On August 19, 1912, Christofferson leapfrogged his new plane through the open span of the Broadway Bridge and under two other Portland bridges before landing on the Willamette River. Later in Seattle, he successfully saved three young men in his hydroplane when their canoe capsized in Lake Washington. On October 27, 1912, Christofferson made the first nighttime hydroplane flight over a city at Coos Bay, Oregon.

Christofferson located the capsized *Osprey*, which was piled up on the north jetty at the mouth of Coos Bay, on November 1, 1912, while flying at six hundred feet. A *Coos Bay Times* reporter accompanied Christofferson in his Curtiss hydroplane while twice attempting to drop a tow line aboard the overturned vessel. They arrived too late to save the five men of the schooner, who were swept overboard into the raging Pacific. At that time, Christofferson considered the fifty-minute flight amid a storm his closest shave with death.

The Christofferson Aviation Company was incorporated in Oregon on December 6, 1912, to construct, purchase and acquire airplanes, biplanes,

"Cusher Pusher Full Scale Replica, 1912." *Pearson Air Museum, Vancouver, Washington.*

hydroplanes and all kinds of aircraft to carry passengers for hire, to conduct schools of aviation and to give flying exhibitions. The company made $96,000 during the first year.

The next year, Christofferson moved his corporate headquarters to Redwood City, California, where he taught the Polar explorer Roald Amundsen how to fly a dual-control plane and sold planes to Amundsen for Arctic exploration. Amundsen erroneously thought that the two planes he bought were flying boats instead of planes capable of landing on smooth ice.

While at San Francisco during a flight, Christofferson pulled out of a dive and was about to land on the bay when a launch pulled out in front of him. To avoid a collision, he capsized the plane. For two long minutes, he was stuck underwater by the waves, held in place by the two shoulder straps by which he steered the bamboo biplane and the four other buckles that held on to the open framework of the kite-like craft.

Silas Christofferson conceived the airplane to be an absolute weapon in modern warfare. He bombed the *South Dakota* battleship with a sandbag to prove that point during the Panama-Pacific International Exposition. This was not on the official program; it occurred when the *South Dakota* entered

San Francisco Bay on November 23, 1913. Christofferson struck the cruiser squarely amidships with his "sand bomb" the first time he tried.

Christofferson went on to "bomb" Seattle, Washington, on July 18, 1914, when the war drums started beating in Europe. He and *Seattle Times* reporter John Evans, acting as bombardier, took twenty-one three-ounce flour sacks as bombs with them as they took off from Lake Washington. Evans dropped the first sack over the lake to see how far the bags would drift due to the wind.

The second sack was dropped over a vacant lot, but the forward momentum of the plane carried it farther and it burst open in a doorway of a house. Evans then calculated 150 feet to where the bombs should land. Their next bomb was dropped near a Ferris wheel at a carnival, with a fifth on a vacant lot in the back of the Washington Hotel.

Christofferson and Evans headed for downtown Seattle after missing a passing ship in Elliott Bay. Evans realized that hitting pedestrians with a small flour sack from one thousand feet could injure someone. He decided to focus on buildings and hit the Rainer-Grand Hotel, breaking a skylight. Next was the Lincoln Hotel and then the waterfront, where a bomb hit the fireboat *Duwamish* and the Star Carriage Building. The final strike hit the Diamond Ice and Storage Company.

Commenting on the Seattle bombing blitz, Christofferson said, "Six airplanes can reduce Seattle to rubble or surrender. The dirigible balloons will be antiquated. There will be nothing left, but the aeroplane armored, equipped with guns, and manned by a crew of adequate scientists. Then must come peace for an aeroplane would be too awful to contemplate."

Despite Christofferson's bombing demonstrations, naval authorities of the time believed that no bomb could be made to pierce the steel armor of a battleship. The army never approved the models of the 1914 competition for an army biplane. The first prize "would not pay even the cost of designing and assembling an aeroplane to comply with the departments requirements," Silas told members of the San Francisco press on July 29, 1914.

Christofferson also said, voicing the feelings of airplane manufacturers, "We feel that the U.S. government will wake up in time. It has been asleep eight years now in aviation matters and it won't be much longer before the public will want to know where the blame belongs."

The navy's contempt for airpower lasted until the early 1920s. Josephus Daniels, the secretary of the navy in 1920, declared that he was willing to stand on a battleship while airplanes attempted to bomb it. Lieutenant C.C. Mosely, later Major Mosely, countered Daniels's offer by volunteering to fly over a warship while all the guns of the naval fleet tried to shoot him down.

"US Navy Flyer JN-4, 1924." *Oregon Historical Society, folder 1059, no. 71215.*

Christofferson is considered one of the best aviators before the Great War. He flew over Mount Whitney on June 23, 1914, setting a U.S. altitude record. He set a long-distance record, flying 306 miles flying from San Francisco to just north of Bakersfield and on to San Diego over the Tehachapi Pass in a one-hundred-horsepower Racine biplane.

Christofferson returned to Portland, Oregon, with his "Aerial Derby" during early August 1914, racing a motorcycle side by side over a three-mile course; he lost because he could not make the turns fast enough. Also, he flew through the open spans of the Broadway drawbridge and filmed footage of the Willamette Falls at Oregon City and the Columbia River Gorge. He did not attempt his famous "Death Dive," where he kills the motor at 2,500 feet and plunges head first toward the ground, because of the air currents that day. "No stunt is dangerous if you get back alive," Silas said.

The Christofferson aircraft company developed a new six-cylinder 117-horsepower engine at 1475rpm with an aluminum block and oil cooler radiator during 1916. The firm sold the planes to Mexico. The new military biplane was constructed from teakwood with silver fittings in an enclosed fuselage and motor. It also was the first plane to feature the stick and rudder control system used in all future planes. On October 21, 1916, one of Christofferson's novice students crashed the plane, receiving fatal injuries.

Christofferson was killed ten days later while evaluating the same plane on October 31. The engine quit at six hundred feet. He dropped one wing in a gentle bank as if to circle the field at three hundred feet. A wing failed to come up. The plane overturned, falling to the ground when the control system failed. Before he died eight hours later, he said, "I got to figure it out."

One biographer wrote in 1932 that "his stunts must not be exaggerated. He was primarily an aeronautical engineer; his designs show steady and significant advancement. He was a silent, methodical laborer for aeronautics."

The Pounder Airport, located on Sandy Boulevard one mile east of Parkrose, was renamed Christofferson Airport on November 1, 1931. His widow, Edna A. Christofferson, spoke and dedicated a plaque. After the brief ceremony, Edna flew solo over the one-hundred-acre airport and adjacent Inverness Golf Course, dropping flowers.

Silas Christofferson was buried at Cypress Lawn Cemetery, San Francisco, besides fellow aviators Lincoln Beachey and Joe Bocquel. The Christofferson Airport lasted less than nine months, serving as a flying field for student pilots for the Adcox School and the National Solo Flying Corporation. Cecil Pounder took back the original name of his airport on July 10, 1932, ending the one tangible reminder of Silas Christofferson in Oregon.

However, his speed and height record of 15,782 feet flying while flying over Mount Whitney and the flight from the rooftop of the Multnomah Hotel in 1912 are remembered. Later, Edwin Bellough made the first landing on

"Silas Christofferson's Curtiss Biplane Atop Multnomah Hotel, June 1912." *Oregon Historical Society, no. 24280.*

the roof of a building in 1919 at Newark, New Jersey. Christofferson made the first demonstration of an airplane bombing a warship on November 23, 1913, and his influence on other aviators whom he trained and inspired remain his legacy to aviation.

JOHNNY "JACK" MAYES: PANCHO VILLA'S AVIATOR

During 1912, Johnny "Jack" Mayes and a friend, Earl Meyer, left Southeast Portland for adventure in California. While living in San Francisco, Mayer met famed aviator Silas Christofferson, who sparked his interest in aviation and taught Mayes how to fly.

Soon after, Mayes headed to Mexico, where he volunteered his flying services to Pancho Villa. However, Villa never intended to use an airplane as a weapon. Instead, Villa hired Mayes as an aerial spy. At Aguascalientes, Mexico, Mayes found a Curtiss biplane that had been cast aside as untrustworthy.

Mayes tinkered with the plane and got it airborne. Flying at sixty miles per hour, the craft suddenly went out of control and crashed into a building, killing him instantly. A newspaper reporter, Floyd Gibbons, wrote, "There beside a wall we buried Jack Mayes." Seven years later, Mayes's mother had the remains of her son disinterred and returned to Portland for burial.

EUGENE ELY: NAVAL PILOT

Eugene Burton Ely's first flight in an aircraft on April 10, 1910, was an accident. Ely, an automobile mechanic from San Francisco, moved to Portland, Oregon, in 1909. Ely, then age twenty-three, seated himself in the Curtiss biplane owned by E. Henry Wemme, the founder of the Portland Aeronautics Club. He started the engine.

The men holding the plane unexpectedly let go as Ely elevated the altitude rudder. In less than ten seconds, the plane was thirty feet in the air. Ely was able to bring it to the grounds of the Rose City Racetrack on Southeast Stark Street after flying two hundred yards, even though it was the first time he ever sat in an airplane.

"Eugene Ely at Rose City Speedway, April 1910." *Oregon Historical Society, no. 24286.*

The next day, Ely made three straight flights in Wemme's plane, exercising an option by the Auburn Automobile dealership to evaluate the plane before buying. On the fourth flight, Ely crashed the plane when a strong northerly wind proved too much as he tried to gain altitude. After reaching a height of thirty feet, the biplane was going into the wind. It reared to the east toward a clump of trees when Ely decided to make a turn in the air for the first time. The north wind caught the sides of the plane and tilted the plane. Seconds later, the pilot and plane hurtled into the ground at thirty miles per hour, making a deep furrow where one of the sides struck.

Wemme was only interested in an airplane to make money at exhibitions for his roadbuilding projects and declined Ely's offer to operate it on a percentage basis. Auburn and Ely bought the plane and transported it to the Curtiss factory at Hammond Port, New York. The plane was adjusted to fit the 165-pound Ely instead of the 125-pound Charles Hamilton, who first flew the plane in Los Angeles, later making the first airplane flight in Oregon on March 5, 1910.

At Salem, Ely raced an automobile and motorcycle as he flew from the state fairgrounds around the Oregon capitol building. Ely had a wreck during the 1910 Rose Festival in June. He was forced to land his plane in a potato field near the Rose City Track when a connecting rod broke, although he escaped uninjured. He made three excellent flights circling downtown Portland and dropping flour sacks on the commercial district. In July, Ely flew in Butte, Montana, and in Manitoba, Canada, where one flight almost killed him.

Ely joined the Curtiss organization and was selected by a drawing to take control of a thirty-five-horsepower Curtiss biplane to enter a contest to fly from Chicago to New York City for a $30,000 prize. He started from Chicago on his one-thousand-mile flight on October 9, 1910, piloting a plane owned by Curtiss, the *Hudson River Flyer*. The flight was aborted due to engine failure. The flight ended the next day at Indiana Harbor, Indiana, only nineteen miles from Chicago. Ely responded to the failure by promising Curtiss, "I will do it again."

Curtiss chose Ely and A.P. McCurdy to race his new plane, a "single surface plane" at Belmont Park, New York. The racing plane had 150 square feet of flying surface compared to 400 square feet of the *Hudson River Flyer* and a sixty-five-horsepower engine with a top speed of more than eighty miles per hour.

Ely became famous for being the first pilot to take off from a ship and land on dry ground on November 14, 1910. He glided from a platform in a Curtiss Model D biplane from the forward deck of the scout ship *Birmingham*, anchored in Chesapeake Bay, descending thirty-seven feet until he touched salt water. Then he rose rapidly and headed eastward five miles to land on the dry beach of the Willough Spit in Virginia.

Ely won an air race held on December 28, 1910, in Los Angeles, piloting a sixty-horsepower Curtiss racer and winning a $5,000 prize by a half a mile. His speed averaged 52 miles per hour during the 8.75-mile race. Ely at this

"Eugene Ely in Plane at Medford, OR, 1911." *Southern Oregon Historical Society, no. 000002.*

"Biplane Taken Off from Medford, OR Field, June 1915." *Southern Oregon Historical Society, no. 000002.*

time was employed by the U.S. government, teaching army officers in San Antonio, Texas. On January 8, 1911, Ely flew at San Francisco, where an angry dog tried to catch him on the runway.

On January 18, 1911, Ely reversed his landmark flight from ship to shore by flying from the racetrack at San Bruno, California, to land on the USS *Pennsylvania*, anchored in San Francisco Bay. Ely used an arresting hook to stop his plane on the landing platform, making the first shipboard landing of an aircraft. After a reception on board the ship, Ely flew from the vessel twenty miles back to the aviation camp. Ely said, "I think the trick could be turned nine times out of ten."

Ely returned to Oregon a national hero, with two Curtiss planes arriving in Medford to make three flawless flights on June 3, 1911. While at Salem, he received $1,000 to race an automobile and motorcycle. He flew from the fairgrounds to circle the state capitol building and returned, where fans swarmed to pencil their names on the wing canvas.

During the Portland Rose Festival on June 6, Ely had three successful flights, circling the city and dropping flour sacks on the business district. After a piston rod problem prevented more flights, Ely said, "I have amassed a considerable fortune, and I would retire now if I could satisfactorily arrange it. There is big money in the game, but it is not worth the while. Something might happen when I am hundreds of feet in the air, there is a possibility and that would be the last of me."

Ely made a flight with his wife, Mabel, at his birthplace of Davenport, Iowa, during early October 1911. On a turn, he was forced to descend. The investigation found that four of the five bolts in one propeller had broken. One local resident asked how long he planned on flying. "Oh, I'll do like the rest of them[,] keep it up until I am killed," he replied.

He was appointed as an aviation instructor for the Coast Artillery Corps. He planned to distribute Curtiss planes on the West Coast after completing the remainder of his contract for the 1911 exhibition tour and then manage a Curtiss flying school in Southern California. He wanted to settle down to the quiet of a home life and the little comforts he so ardently longed for but could not have while traveling across North America.

Eugene Ely fell to his death fifty feet in a crash in Macon, Georgia, on October 19, 1911, the next-to-last exhibition on his 1911 schedule. He was the eighty-fifth aviator to die in just two years. His last words were, "I lost control. I am going to die."

It was a tragic ending to a short career, climaxing in being the first pilot to take off from a ship deck and land on dry ground and reversing his historical flight in 1911 by taking off from dry ground and landing on a warship. He posthumously received the U.S. Distinguished Flying Cross.

There is a purpose, beyond money and thrills for an audience, in performing death-defying acts. Often flying has military applications, rather than simply showing how close to killing oneself an aviator can come without doing it. Eugene Ely did both.

Charles Walsh:
One of Many Who Met a Tragic End

Charles Francis Walsh was born on October 27, 1877, in Mission Valley, California. The family moved to San Diego, where Lincoln Beachey trained him. Walsh crashed his own monoplane, built out of seasoned spruce and piano wire, in San Diego on January 23, 1910; parts of the forty-foot-long frame and fifty-foot wingspan were thrown into the crowd, but no one was seriously injured. Walsh taxied his airplane into a fence to avoid hitting a Curtiss plane piloted by Charles Hamilton.

H.W. Manning, the founder of the Pacific Aircraft Company, signed Walsh during April 1911, and the pair headed for Victoria, British Columbia, accompanied by a Curtiss-Farman biplane during the Easter weekend. The next week at Wenatchee, Washington, Walsh crashed it into an apple tree.

Walsh flew for the benefit of friends, the officials of Rose Festival Association and the press at the Portland Country Club fairgrounds on May 7, 1911. He refused an offer to fly to Baker City, Oregon, or St. Louis during the Fourth of July holiday but went instead to Roseburg on May 11–12, 1911, for a flight exhibition.

Walsh returned to Portland and flew his forty-foot-wingspan Curtiss-Farman biplane based on a Curtiss design, with a fifty-horsepower motor, on May 21, 1911, for eight minutes. A two-bladed propeller of eight and a half feet diameter, rotating at 1200rpm, was directly connected to the motor. Walsh added silver dust to the unbleached muslin, the plane becoming known as the "American Silver Dart." The Curtiss-style ailerons located between the upper and lower wings were a Farman type, mounted flush to the end of all four wings.

On May 28, 1911, at the Portland Club fairgrounds, Walsh flew for more than fifteen minutes, fourteen miles over Southeast Portland, outdistancing Charles Hamilton. Later that day, Walsh lost an automobile race to a Ford racer before a crowd of four thousand spectators. Jack and Brownie Manning and Walsh departed for Victoria, British Columbia, on May 30, 1911, for an aviation exhibition.

On June 11, 1911, Walsh lost control of his plane in a "whirlpools of wind," landing in a tangle of telephone wires just short of the landing site at Madison Park in Seattle, destroying the plane. Walsh escaped uninjured.

The Walsh plane weighed between 1,100 and 1,350 pounds, and its speed was thirty-seven miles per hour; 21 pounds were lifted per horsepower and 2.8 pounds per surface foot. The aspect ratio is 5 to 1.

The seats for the aviator and passenger were on the front of the lower plane. The directional rudder was a Henri Farman design, placed in the rear, comprising two equal vertical-placed surfaces of thirty feet square each. A hinged foot lever, its center connected to the two rudders by cables, controlled the direction left or right.

Walsh conducted his first passenger flight carrying *Oregonian* reporter Roscoe Fawcett. The journalist wrote, "The sensation of aero planing is much like auto mobile riding with the bumps and bruises left out." The good reporter never feared a crash into the ground. He went on to write that the plane "mounted gracefully into the air after skimming along the ground for 100 feet and for the next few seconds the grass faded away into one green kaleidoscope."

Three days later, the first woman airplane passenger in Oregon, actress Vida Perrin, was escorted aloft. Ms. Perrin was surprised by Walsh's calm demeanor. She said, "Most of the time Mr. Walsh was chatting with me, unconcernedly as starting an automobile trip."

The lack of air currents caused Walsh to dive from an altitude of fifty feet at La Grande, Oregon, on July 8, 1911. The machine tilted upward and, without warning, dove downward, careening and swerving like a tail-less kite. Walsh said that "he had struck a seeming vacuum in the air." Walsh had no control except for an instant when he dodged the roof of a house four city blocks from the takeoff site, swerving left into a tree, which saved him from a more severe injury. Next the plane turned end to end and came down with a crash that left it in a twisted mass of junk, including a broken propeller. The engine, at least, was intact. A frightened crowd found Walsh thrown from the pilot seat by the impact with the tree.

At Laramie, Wyoming, Walsh set the American altitude record of 7,200 feet on July 31, 1911. He left the Manning Organization over a contract dispute of $56.25 in ticket sales at Fremont, Nebraska, which ended in a fistfight with Manning in front of the Terry Hotel.

Walsh talked about flying and the faith he had in his airplanes. "I never feel at all nervous or frightened. If a fellow follows his machine and has the requisite nerve he would never be injured very badly."

Soon afterward, Walsh joined the Curtiss team, flying his newly assigned seventy-five-horsepower Curtiss Pusher at Sterling, Illinois, on August 31, 1911. Walsh, age twenty-six, was killed in a spiral descent of two thousand feet at an exhibition at Trenton, New Jersey, on October 2, 1912, proving that even the best aviators could be killed at any time.

ROUND THE RIM FLYERS

The Round the Rim Flyers left Washington, D.C., on July 24, 1919, going north at 113 miles per hour on their first stop at Augusta, Maine. The purpose of the flight around the borders or rims of the forty-eight contiguous states was to map future air routes and landing spots and evaluate the 873-horsepower Liberty motors and stability devices.

Lieutenant Colonel R.F. Hartz, Sergeant Jerry Doblas, Lieutenant Ernest E. Hamon and Sergeant Jack Harding flew in a Liberty Glenn Martin bomber, which had a forty-four-foot wingspan and a forty-four-foot length. The crew flew west to Cleveland, Chicago and Milwaukie, Wisconsin, on September 27, 1919. They arrived at Missoula, Montana, on November 1, where they were delayed by a blizzard before flying westward to Coeur d'Alene, Idaho.

When reaching the Pacific Northwest, the flyers were the first to circle Mount Rainier. The flyers then landed at Seattle, Tacoma, Portland and San Francisco. Later stops in Texas were at El Paso and Dallas on November 1, 1919.

The main problem facing the aviators, besides storms, was the low air pressure at ten thousand to twelve thousand feet, which can blow out the landing gear of overinflated tires when the inside pressure of the tires exceeds the outside pressure of the atmosphere. However, the crew never experienced a blowout. The ten-thousand-mile flight ended on November 9, 1919, back at Boling Field near the nation's capital. The total time in the air was 114 hours, 45 minutes.

AROUND THE WORLD FLYERS

Lieutenant Lowell H. Smith, a resident from Eugene, Oregon, and commander of the U.S. Army Aerial Expedition, along with five other aviators, completed the first circumnavigation of the world by air, landing on the shore of Lake Washington northeast of Seattle on September 28, 1924. The other five aviators were Lieutenant Leigh P. Wade, Eric H. Nelson, Leslie Arnold, Henry H. Odgen and Lieutenant John Harding Jr.

The flight began from Clover Field in Santa Monica, California, on March 17, 1924, in four single-engine open-cockpit Douglas World Cruisers (DWC). The fuel capacity of the DWC was 644 gallons. The U.S. Army viewed the trip north along the Pacific shore from Southern California to Seattle as a mere trial flight to see if its planes were satisfactory. Before their arrival at Seattle, the world flight insignias were not painted or named.

The four planes were named for great American cities: *Chicago*, *Boston*, *Seattle* and *New Orleans*. The first landing heading north was Sacramento, California, followed by the second at Eugene, Oregon, on March 15, 1924. There was a brief layover in Vancouver, Washington.

The commander of the flight was Frederick Martin. Captain Lowell H. Smith and Lieutenant Leigh P. Wade were the first to land at Vancouver. Then Wade and Smith took off and circled south to Portland for fifteen minutes before flying on to Seattle. Three thousand people saw the landing at Pearson Field. The commander at the Vancouver Barracks, the mayors of

"U.S. World Fliers; The New Orleans at Medford, OR, October 24, 1924." *Southern Oregon Historical Society, no. 016682.*

Portland and Vancouver and both chambers of commerce greeted the flyers after their landing. The flyers were whisked away to attend a brief luncheon in their honor at the Benson Hotel in Portland.

The four planes were in Seattle at the Sand Point Field from March 20 until April 6, 1924, where the landing gears were removed and replaced with giant pontoons. The flyers never considered that they were on a long journey until they hopped off from Seattle, leaving the United States for a water landing in the harbor of Prince Rupert, British Columbia.

"The interesting and most dangerous part of our trip starts from Seattle. This is where we began. Anyone can fly to Seattle" from Santa Monica, California. "From now on we were pioneers and will be called to do our best," said Lieutenant Smith.

The northern portion of the flight was more feared by aviators than any other part of the journey due to climate, isolated towns and long supply lines. Emergency rafts at each water landing from Alaska to Kolkata (Calcutta), India, were available upon water landings, tied to big mooring buoys within the harbors of Alaska, Japan and Shanghai, China. The pontoons remained on the planes until they reached Kolkata, India, where landing wheels were installed.

The rafts, constructed of four barrels of steel drums, were fastened together as a float and made available by towing whenever a pontoon leaked, preventing the sinking of the plane. The rafts were available for towing to any of the four planes. The emergency rafts were supplemented by four five-hundred-pound anchors, available in sheltered water and connected by a heavy cable to a floating buoy of steel drums painted yellow.

The most dangerous part of the flight centered on the Aleutian Islands. Major Frederick Martin and Sergeant Alva L. Harvey left Chignik and wrecked their plane *Seattle* on a mountainside of Attu Island on April 30, 1924. They walked into the Pacific American Fisheries Station ten days later, never to rejoin the flight.

"Lt. Smith, commander of the flight. Do not delay longer waiting for Major Martin," read the message from the chief of the air service on May 2, 1924. "See that everything possible is done to find him. Planes two, three, and four to proceed to Japan at earliest moment."

Lowell Smith was the perfect aviator to replace Major Martin. He and Lieutenant John P. Richter were the first pilots to complete an air refueling maneuver in flight on July 27, 1923, setting an endurance record of more than thirty-seven hours, as well as distance and speed records.

The 878-mile flight from Attu Island across the Bering Sea southeast to the Kuril Islands off Japan was the longest leg of their journey up to that point. The six aviators arrived in Tokyo on May 23, 1924. They were honored with a medal from the emperor of Japan for the first transpacific crossing.

Lieutenant Smith flew his plane south to Tourane, Indochina, and east to Bangkok, Thailand, with a new airplane engine. During his stay at Rangoon, British India, on June 21, 1924, he suffered an intestinal disorder, delaying the flight; a cargo boat also collided with one of the U.S. Army planes, severely damaging the wings. When flying over the Bay of Bengal, the army team defeated the "Jinx of the Akyab," the name for the monsoons between Yangon (Rangoon) and Kolkata, India.

The War Department commissioned Lowell Thomas to aid the flyers in writing their accounts of their globe-encircling journey in the air. Thomas called them the "Magellan's of the Air." Eric Nelson told Thomas, "Although our long, long trip was not officially to come to an end until we reached Seattle, nevertheless at the onset of our trip we had flown our Douglas Cruisers down to San Diego to get the instruments adjusted therefore if we could reach Rockwell Field, Coronado we knew no matter what happened to the rest of our flight from there on up the Pacific coast, we would have flown the entire distance around the world. So, this day's flight was the one that to bring all our dreams true."

The flyers arrived at San Diego, where Rear Admiral Ashley Robinson said, "Other men will fly around the earth. Never again will anybody fly around the world for the first time." The starting point at Clover Field, Santa Monica, California, on September 23, 1924, was reached after flying 25,583 miles around the world.

General Patrick ordered the aviators to continue their World Cruisers flight north for their final disposal at Seattle. The aviators attended a banquet and dance in Sacramento. Lieutenant Oakley G. Kelly, the commander at Pearson Field, headed an escort of six planes, taking off from the field at the Vancouver Barracks and flying south to greet the three Douglas air cruisers on September 27, 1924, where a throng of four thousand people were already gathered at the original Eugene airport at the corner of West Nineteenth Avenue and Chambers Street.

Eugene was where Lieutenant Smith once flew for the Fire Patrol Service and where his parents lived. One day, while Lieutenant Smith was on patrol, he spotted a fire, and when he tried to report it, he found the radio "on the blink." He crawled out on to the wings while his pilotless plane dropped downward; he fixed the radio and returned to the cockpit. "Had to report the fire," he said.

There was an evening banquet at the Osbourne Hotel attended by three hundred people. Smith confided to a friendly reporter that he was weary of all the banquets and crowds. "This public stuff is the bunk. I long for a chance to get away with my own friends, to spend a little time at ease. It is no fun to be rubbed at like a chimpanzee in a cage. Prizefight[er]s and stage stars eat it up, but not yours truly."

The escort planes led by the global girdlers flew north to circle the city of Portland before landing at Vancouver, where the flyers spoke before the crowd of well-wishers. Lieutenant Smith said, "The greatest reward we had during our flight, and our greatest reward now, is in the knowledge that the American people are pulling for us and our branch of the service and in knowing our little effort has been appreciated."

Mayor George Baker of Portland complained that "Eugene has a flying field, Vancouver has a flying field, and the other cities in the Northwest are similarly equipped but the only things that fly which can a landing in Portland are ducks and geese."

The world flyers were later guests at the Multnomah Hotel. The chamber of commerce and the Advertising Club gave the dinner. Each of the flyers received Pendleton and Oregon City blankets as a "token of warmth."

"Portland Mayor George Baker: Cutout Picture Taken at Council Crest Amusement Park."
Oregon Historical Society, folder 1059, negative 49690.

The world flyers arrived at Eugene for the third time, quietly, on October 18, 1924. They went on a deer hunting trip on the Mackenzie River with friends. The group told their stories to Lowell Thomas inside a Cascade Mountain cabin around the fireplace. Thomas gave them nicknames to humanize them, like "Smiling Jack" Harding and "Silent" Lowell Smith because of his short and cryptic sentences. Few people were present to witness their final departure from Eugene south to Sacramento, San Francisco, and Santa Monica, California.

Lowell Thomas compared the six American aviators to the captains of the great sailing explorers of the 1500s like Vasco de Gama, Magellan and Sir Francis Drake. C.G. Gray, the editor of the British magazine *The Aeroplane*, wrote in 1924 that along with the Wright brothers and the first flyers to cross the Atlantic, "it is an accord with precedent that an American team should be the first to circle the globe."

Zenith Carburetors ran ads after the flight during January 1925 that it produced the "carburetors of the world flyers." Few individuals recall today these six American flyers of 1924 and their flight.

Unlike maritime sailors of old, these flyers did not fly into the unknown. They had naval support, established bases for supplies, weather reports and a budget of $5 million. The spare parts included fifteen Liberty engines, fourteen extra pontoons and two airframes. Only two planes, the flagship *Chicago*, piloted by Lieutenant Lowell Smith along with mechanic Lieutenant Arnold, and the *New Orleans*, piloted by Eric Nelson and John Harding, fully circled the globe. The planes received new engines at Karachi, India, and again at San Diego prior to their return to Seattle.

The plane *Boston* had to make a forced landing off the coast of Scotland on August 4, 1924, due to engine trouble. The pilot, Leigh Wade, was picked up by the USS *Richmond*. The *Boston* was declared beyond repair during the attempt to hoist it aboard the cruiser and was replaced by the *Boston II* at Pictou, Nova Scotia, where all four planes flew southward to Boston.

Crossing the Alleghenies was the second-most difficult part remaining of their homeward journey. If an airplane motor freezes up, the crew could crack up on a mountain top. West of Harpers Ferry, West Virginia, the five escort planes encountered fog. They returned to Washington, D.C., while the world flyers went on relying on good fortune.

It was not possible for the planes to exceed 6,500 feet in elevation due to the strains put on the planes during the long journey, and so a southern route was chosen. The safer route was southwest from St. Joseph, Missouri, to Dallas, Texas, to avoid the highest section of the Rocky Mountains while flying westward to San Diego at the lowest possible altitude.

History records the dates and names of those Americans who first circled the planet in airplanes, traveling 26,345 miles in sixty-six days of actual flying after the British failed attempt in 1922. In 1923, the French tried. During 1924, Italy, Portugal and Britain announced plans to circle the globe. The distance is more than 25,000 miles around the world at the equator. During 1930, Austrian Charles Kingston Smith and three others completed the first circumnavigation while crossing the equator twice.

Most remembered are the first Americans who crossed the Atlantic by air in 1919 and the two British flyers who flew nonstop across the Atlantic three weeks later. The public is hardly aware of Lowell Smith and the other aviators and their first circumnavigation. The most enduring memorial are the memorial and plaque at the Magnuson Park entrance at Northeast Seventy-Fourth Street in Seattle, Washington.

All six airmen were awarded the Distinguished Service medal, the first time the medal was given in peacetime for aviation endeavors. Fredrick Martin was later in command of the army aviation unit in Hawaii during the attack on Pearl Harbor. Alva L. Harvey, the mechanic, became commander of heavy bomber groups during World War II. Eric Nelson became a colonel, working on the development and operational deployment of the B-29 Superfortress.

Other aviators are more famous and remembered than Lieutenant Lowell Howard Smith, such as Charles Lindbergh, Howard Hughes, Wiley Post and Amelia Earhart. Three Soviet men flew in a single plane across the North Pole in 1937 to Vancouver, Washington, piloted by Valery Chkalov. The Russian crew paved the way for transpolar flights and is famous in the Pacific Northwest.

CHAPTER 6

AVIATION COMPANIES

THE PACIFIC AVIATION COMPANY

H.W. Manning, a Portland gas mantle manufacturer, and his three sons built three airplanes called the "Comets." The Pacific Aviation Company incorporated at Southwest 623 Oak Street during 1910 to build dirigibles and accessories for machines used in aerial navigation and for their stability.

Jack Manning suffered an accident that crushed his fingers in a plane's engine even before his first flight in the plane he built at the rear of his father's electrical shop at 48 Third Street. Later, Frank Manning made test flights in *Comet I* but wanted a larger plane; he bought one from J.M. Rache of New York. The Manning family contracted to make four flights during the 1910 Rose Festival, but the plane *Comet II* was not ready. However, their flying grounds, three planes that were covered with canvas cloth and a school at the Rose City Speedway at Twelve Mile House on Southeast Stark Street were operational.

During summer, *Comet II* made one good flight at Astoria not mentioned in the local newspapers. Manning hired Bruno Seibel, a Los Angeles race car driver known as the "Flying Dutchman," as a pilot. Seibel crashed near Tacoma, Washington, on August 10, 1910, suffering no broken bones but being left with marks imprinted on his chest from the steering wheel. Seibel blamed himself for making too abrupt a turn; the airplane dove so fast that he was unable to right it up in time, and the result was a fall of eighty feet.

"I will be out in a couple of days and intend to fly again try it again," said Seibel. "I think Manning has solved the aeroplane problem, for the machine I had is one of the fastest I ever tried."

H.W. Manning transported Seibel back to Portland to recover at the family residence on the west side of the 2600 block of Northwest Savier Street. Manning prohibited his three sons from further flying and even threatened to sell his eighty-three-horsepower engine and plane to N.A. Brown of Tacoma, who was constructing a Bleriot racing monoplane.

During May 1911, Manning signed up California aviator Charles F. Walsh, who headed for Victoria accompanied by the Mannings. Manning purchased a Curtiss-Farman biplane sporting an eighty-three-horsepower motor and headed next to Wenatchee, Washington, where Walsh crashed into an apple tree.

Also signed up by Manning was aviator J.W. Depries from Sutherlin, Oregon, who constructed a fifty-horsepower Curtiss biplane and flew to Long Beach, Washington, during the summer of 1910. He also flew over Roseburg during May 10–11, 1911. Depries later was a suspect in the disappearance of a plane from a country club in Sutherlin and gave up aviation soon after leaving the state. He later went into the automobile industry manufacturing carburetors in Portland in 1921.

The elder Manning imposed a flying ban on his three sons. Manning kept Seibel, De Preis and Walsh on as pilots and transported the plane back to Portland, where Walsh made the first passenger flight; three days later, the first woman was carried aloft in Oregon. When asked about not being allowed to fly, Jack Manning said, "We leave that to Charlie."

The *Morning Astorian* printed the Manning's Company future intentions in a series of ads along with a story of a good flight made during the summer of 1911. Charles Walsh experimented with an invention sponsored by Manning, the Ellsworth equilibrator, to help aircraft maintain lateral balance at the artillery grounds of Fort Vancouver, Washington, beginning on June 29, 1911. The two identical devices, on each side of the biplane, limit tipping to five degrees. A pendulum hangs plumb, and should the airplane dip, one of the two little plungers attached to the pendulum dip into a mercury solution or contact switch, which then sets an electromagnetic clutch; this operates two drums that, in turn, tilt up or down, as necessary, to right the aircraft to level. Afterward, lateral flight electromagnets turned the clamps off.

A great barrier to long-distance flights has been the constant strain of keeping an airplane balanced horizontally. The only way of doing this at the time was by swaying the body from side to side, but hours of this physical strain leave the operators in a weakened physical and mental condition. Walsh evaluated the equilibrator at the 1911 International Aviation Meet at Chicago, held August 12–20. Days later, Walsh left the Manning Organization over a contract dispute of $56.25 in ticket sales at Fremont, Nebraska.

During October 1911, Manning formed the Swastika Mining Company, located five miles from Lakeview, Idaho, selling shares in a gold and silver mine. He assigned the equilibrator U.S. patent No. 1024398A, granted on December 12, 1910, to C.E. Huston and H.L. Lane. Manning developed a new plane without the front planes and hired Silas Christofferson to evaluate it by flying over Vancouver, Washington.

Manning gave up aviation in 1913 and continued his lighting business in Portland. He invented a portable gas stove for campers in 1917. The Manning Lighting and Supply Company, located at 223 Southwest Sixth Avenue, was last mentioned in the 1931 issue of the *Oregonian*.

REKAR AIRSHIP COMPANY

John J. Rekar of San Francisco started the Rekar Airship Company when his patent 922,952A was granted on May 25, 1909, for an airship. His partner, Edward P. Preble, the president of Vancouver Ice and Storage, financed the venture. The pair planned to construct a dirigible capable of traveling with five passengers from Portland to Los Angeles in seven hours. The passenger cabin was suspended seven feet beneath the main frame.

The 206-foot-long-by-24-foot-wide frame tapered to a wedge at both ends and was constructed out of strips of Oregon spruce fastened by copper piano wire by forty carpenters and wood joiners. The strips of wood were an inch in width and a quarter-inch thick; these laminated strips for aircraft saw use years before Howard Hughes and his birch strips of the *Spruce Goose*. The covering, engine parts and frame were held within the vacated horticultural building of the Lewis and Clark Exhibition of 1905. The seven gas bags were built into separate compartments so that if any deflated, the dirigible would remain aloft. The five thirty-five-horsepower engines turned the five-foot diameter helicopter blades at 1000rpm, providing all lift since the dirigible contained no ballast.

A nonfabric material covered the airship. Five engines costing $5,000 were assembled. The work halted when it was realized that the firm owed

$950 in judgements. The company was incorporated in Oregon on January 30, 1910, with a capital stock of $500,000. Preble was considering an offer from the Russian government for $3 million whenever the airship proved capable of flying one thousand miles.

Rekar and Preble were sued for attorney fees of $790.50 during July 1910 because their company lacked funds. The world fair building, containing the airframe and engines, was razed during September 1910. The airship was not completed, and the airframe's fate is lost to history.

Long Airplane Works

The parents of the Long brothers bought the homestead in 1887 and raised four boys, who operated the two-hundred-acre farm, constructed airplanes, wood propellers, radios and engaged in a lengthy list of other distinct activities, including running a flight school.

Leslie Long, airplane designer and builder, never went up in a plane. There is a bust of Long in Wisconsin at the museum of the Experimental Aircraft Association, where he is regarded as a pioneer, and he was a member of the Oregon Aviation Hall of Fame and head of the Light Plane Association of America for three years from 1932 to 1935.

Pictures of Les Long taken in 1938 by the *Oregonian* show a thin, forty-eight-year-old man with a prominent nose and dark horn-rimmed glasses. Mike Parker of the Northwest Vintage Radio Society described Les as "rather dapper."

Due to his busy workload, as well as his agoraphobia, Long did not leave the family farm over the course of twenty-five years. Recognizing that an attack of the Spanish flu pandemic in 1918 had left him of incapable of engaging in the strenuous labor of farming, Long turned to other economic enterprises for money.

"I like to fool with things that that require exactness," he explained. So, he began to whittle airplane propellers. He built a glider in 1910 and a telescope, and as a boy in school, he bought and read every book on aeronautics that he could find.

When an aviator landed his ship alongside the family house in 1927, Leslie decided that he would build airplanes. He started that same night, using the family radio shop. The plane was completed during October 1929 and had a twenty-five-horsepower motor, could reach a speed of ninety miles per hour, weighed 425 pounds, had a millage of thirty-five miles per gallon and sold for $1,200; it was the first airplane constructed in Washington County.

The different "Longster" models became the successors to the five-tube battery-powered radios made by the Long Radio Works, established in 1912 after Leslie constructed a variometer. The radio service business was left in 1927 to brother George Long, the "radio repairman." The radio repair and Crosley retail store was located at Long Airport, one mile north of Cornelius, on Rural Route 1, later renamed Long Road after the family farm.

Over the next sixteen years, Long designed and built eleven planes weighing more than 425 pounds, which became known as "light planes," adapted from larger mail planes called the "Longster." In comparison, ultra-lights are just powered gliders and weigh less than 1,400 pounds, while his designer planes contained a cockpit housing the pilot. He invented a light plane, the low wing "Longster," and innovated the homebuilt airplane industry by selling kits. His plans appeared in *Modern Mechanixs and Inventions* and *Sportsman Aviation* magazines. His plans are still sold as reprints.

The Hi-Low has slightly bent wings instead of being straight like the wings of a gulf or swan. Eastern experts in the 1930s predicted that the plane might establish a modern style in airplane building. Long concluded that there are only practical designs for light low wing planes—the cantilever and the wire-braced types. Since the cantilever is too difficult for an amateur to attempt, being like a pre-stressed steel or wood beam, Long went ahead with the wire-braced low wing.

The wire-braced low wings are easy to fly and build compared to high wings. In addition, low wings are faster and have lower landing speed, quicker takeoff and better visibility for the pilot. In retrospect, this seems obvious, as racing, military and commercial planes are also low wings. The low wing design was valuable for amateurs given their safety, ease of construction and low cost.

The Long brothers rebuilt Henderson and the eighty-horsepower Anziani motorcycle engines, adapting them for use, as well as the Long Harlequin, a thirty-five-horsepower motor weighing ninety pounds of Long's own design. Harley Davidson engines were adapted to aviation using the two Harley pistons, cylinders and connecting rods, while Les Long produced the new crankshaft and an aluminum crankcase.

All Longsters are easier to fly for everyone except commercial pilots, who are familiar only with larger planes and more power. A pilot from West Coast Airlines was unable to lift off on the much shorter Cornelius airstrip compared to commercial airports, bringing the high wing Longster he was evaluating to a quick stop by way of a telephone pole. The pilot was uninjured, but the propeller was ruined.

The Henderson Longster designed in 1933 was the Long brothers' most famous plane. The brothers lightened the Anziani Longster for use with Henderson motorcycle engines. Its air speed was seventy-five miles per hour at 2850rpm. It had a good steep climbing angle to four thousand feet and could land at twenty-five miles per hour in still air. The glide angle was fully 12 to 1.

The Long brothers also started and operated a flying school. Ed Bell conducted the school and worked in the propeller shop. Leslie refused offers to go into large-scale production of the propellers. He labored as a highly skilled craftsman, turning out propellers made entirely by hand and doing clerical work for his four brothers.

Long's last plane design was the open-cockpit Wimpy, powered by a twenty-seven-horsepower Aeronca engine or a forty-horsepower Continental. It had a welded fuselage; external wire bracing, attached to a fitting behind the tire of each; tail feathers; and a wooden wing with a span of 31.5 feet and length of 12 feet. The Wimpy design came to influence all future homebuilt airplanes after World War II.

"'Wimpy' Model Airplane, Circa 1940 Designed by Leslie Long." *Oregon Historical Society, folder 1059, negative 27207.*

The Long airplane business faced a decline in the late 1930s. The great hope for the future of aviation, according to Les Long, was his students at the Long School of Flying, as well as helpers who came to the family farm in droves aiding in welding and painting. Long wrote that "neither Orville nor Wilbur Wright was licensed by Federal or State authorities. Yet it was they who launched the flimsy glider at Kitty Hawk."

One dealer experienced a 90 percent reduction in sales of light plane kits over ten years ending in 1937; 75 percent of the state laws based on the Uniform State Flying Law restricted the use of homebuilt aircraft. An exception was the two-hundred-acre Springfield Municipal Airport, which welcomed homebuilt planes. Les Long flew Longsters at the Private Flyers Association, held there on April 16–17, 1938, and so did Charles Bernard of Beaverton.

The Oregon Department of Aviation, founded on February 11, 1921, was the first governmental aviation department in the United States, and Oregon was the only state that did not restrict homebuilt craft and inspected amateur planes while under construction.

Les Long wrote in *Popular Aviation* that he blamed his lost business on the Depression and big business aided by federal regulation. It became easier for thousands of young men to give up their hobby instead of being "down in the basement making up a set of Clark Y rigs; [they are] out on the roads, trying to wrap dad's sedan around a telegraph pole."

The Long brothers tried to make more money by expanding the air service. By 1935, the Long Air Service had four planes in service, including a Taylor Cub. The planes were available for regular student instruction and charter trips anywhere on short notice. The Oregon coast became a destination point at only fifty minutes' travel from Cornelius. It is doubtful that this endeavor made money during the Great Depression.

George Bogardus of Troutdale, Oregon, an Oregon Aviation Hall of Fame inductee, bought a Wimpy after the Second World War that was in storage, renaming it the *Little Bee Gee*, and got it certified in 1947. He added a canopy, a new tail and cowling. He then flew the *Little Bee Gee* from Oregon to Washington, D.C., in 1948 to lobby the Civilian Aviation Authority for the establishment of the "experimental/amateur built" license category, which was successful.

The Federal Aviation Administration (FAA), successor to the CAA, added an experimental class of license for noncommercial recreational purposes such as educational and personal class use due in part to Bogardus's flight of Long's Wimpy. Les Long's dream of federal licensing of homebuilt aircraft based on the Oregon model became his legacy.

Long discovered the "burble effect," which is the turbulence between an airplane wing and fuselage. This was realized by a man who had never flown in an airplane. Whenever a plane was flown for the first time, Long would go into his bedroom and cover his head with blankets on the bed in fear of its failure, according to biographer George Bogardus.

Long discovered that it wasn't just airplanes that required propellers in western Oregon. Fruit dryers outsold airplane propellers ten to one for canneries due to vinegar flies being present. The Long radio business and propeller manufacturing remained a family enterprise. Leslie Long refused offers to go into large-scale production because he always considered himself a craftsman, preferring to carve propellers by hand.

The Long Radio Works business was still in business in 1942, although no AC-powered radios were built, nor battery-powered tuned radio frequency (TRF) radios after 1927. The last radios assembled by Long were an eight-tube superheterodyne Model S-8 and radio kits. The Long Radio Works, like all other manufacturers, ended all hopes of radio construction when the government shut down civilian production at the start of World War II. The remaining radio parts on hand like transformers, wire and switches were used by George and Les Long to assemble electric fence chargers, their last product up to the time of Les Long's death in 1945; afterward, George Long continued to repair radios.

THE BOEING AIRPLANE COMPANY

William E. Boeing, millionaire lumberman from Seattle, Washington, presented a $10,000 hydroplane to the Northwest Aero Club in 1915 that later almost sank on Lake Washington. The supply of spruce lumber and the access to capital are two reasons the Boeing Airplane Company began in Seattle.

Boeing was incorporated on July 15, 1916. Boeing wanted to learn to fly before building airplanes. The first plane, the model B&W, was constructed in a former barn near Lake Washington that stood for the founders' surnames, Boeing and Conrad Westervelt. The company became a million-dollar concern in 1919 employing twenty-one men after receiving a fifty-plane contract from the U.S. government.

On April 12, 1921, Boeing won a $1.4 million U.S. government contract for two hundred Thomas Morse–type pursuit planes and for remodeling fifty existing De Havilland army airplanes. During the lean years of 1922 and 1923, William Boeing returned to the manufacturing of furniture.

Six years later, the U.S. government contract for airmail and passenger service rights between San Francisco and Chicago was won by Boeing and announced on January 29, 1927. Vern G. Gorst of the Pacific Air Transport company, an early rival of Boeing's before their 1928 merger, said, "The Boeing Company is a capable organization and is certain to succeed in giving fast airmail and passenger service on the 1900-mile stretch. Then it, too, is a Northwest firm."

Boeing made a flying office, selling it for $25,000. The pilot had to brave the weather in an open cockpit while cruising at one hundred miles per hour. The enclosed cabin of the Boeing 40B4 had space for two passengers, an electric starter, land lights that fold into the wings, parachutes, flares and an engine fire suppression system. This tri-motor plane was almost identical to the mail planes used by Pacific Air Transport, a partner of Boeing and United Airlines in 1931.

William Boeing became chairman of the board for United Aircraft Transport on December 6, 1928, the biggest aircraft corporation of the world, which owned the Boeing brand. In 1934, William E. Boeing retired after losing control of his original company.

The Boeing brand became known worldwide when the company, beginning in 1935, manufactured at Seattle a bomber, based on the design of all-metal two-engine Boeing 247 Transport. The three Boeing plants at Seattle and the Wichita, Kansas, assembly plant manufactured the B-17 Flying Fortress bomber.

The B-17 was powered by four 1200-horsepower motors, with a speed of three hundred miles per hour and a cruising range of three thousand miles. The Boeing B-24 and B-25 bombers were built during the Second World War.

Pacific Air Transport and United

Vern C. Gorst of North Bend, Oregon, and his son advertised circa 1913 that he was ready to carry passengers across Coos Bay with a Martin hydroplane they assembled and learned to fly. This could have been the first air service advertised anywhere. The service folded because of a lack of passengers and fanfare.

Pacific Airline passenger blanket, circa 1930. *Photo by Murray N. Stone.*

The Pacific Air Transport Company, forerunner of United Airlines, incorporated in January 1926 in Portland with Vern Gorst as president. The company won an airmail contract for delivery from Seattle via Portland to Los Angeles. Eight Ryan single-engine airplanes were ordered from San Diego, and twelve pilots were hired.

Vernon Bookwalter flew the first official airmail out of Pearson Field south to Medford on September 15, 1926. He took off with six thousand letters weighing 184 pounds in a Ryan M-1 biplane and returned to Vancouver with mail from Medford and California. Grover Tyler continued the last leg of the mail flight to Seattle.

The Pacific Coast airmail route between Seattle and Los Angeles, with stops at Vancouver and Medford, made a good profit in 1927 for Pacific Air Transport. During 1928, the transport company moved from Pearson Field in Vancouver to the newly completed airport at Swan Island in Portland. Mail delivery to the Medford Municipal Airport, with its new five-thousand-foot runway, began on October 3, 1929.

The first air service eastward from the Pacific Northwest began when Varney Airlines founder Walter T. Varney started flights from Pasco, Washington, to Boise, Idaho, on April 26, 1926. Later flights from Elko, Nevada, to Salt Lake City, Utah, began on June 1, 1926. Varney established his east divisional headquarters at Boise on March 1, 1930, bringing six pilots from the Pasco airport.

The planes of the Pacific Air Transport Company were equipped to send and receive voice messages by November 1929. Weather broadcast from the

"First Airmail Flight Out of Medford, 1926." *Southern Oregon Historical Society, no. 000004.*

U.S. Weather Bureau on Swan Island and orders and messages from the company comprised the broadcasts to the airborne transport. L.G. Hubble was the district superintendent of the Pacific airmail, express and passenger service during the 1930s.

Roy Warner was flying at 7,500 feet carrying the mail on the Pasco, Washington, to Boise, Idaho, portion of the airmail route from Salt Lake City to Portland. The plane developed a fuel line leak near Baker City, Oregon, and he was able to cut the engine. Suddenly a fire broke out and flames shot back, setting his pants on fire and burning his hand while he grasped the stick.

During his landing approach, the fire spread and burned the fabric of the right wing. The airplane spun around, bounced into the air and came to a stop right side up with the cockpit in flames. Warner jumped out grasping for fresh air. He thought of the mail and rushed back to the burning plane, throwing all the mail bags to the ground, before the gas tank exploded and the plane was engulfed in a ball of fire.

Warner's clothes were partially burned off, his hands were blistered and bleeding and his eyebrows and eyelashes were gone. He was still standing and somehow flew on to Pasco to deliver the mail. For his dedication to duty, he was awarded the Air Mail Medal of Honor by the U.S. Postal Service, its highest award.

On September 21, 1931, Warner performed another public service—this time, he saved a forest. He spotted a small forest fire while crossing the Blue Mountains and circled around it, attracting the attention of a forest ranger who was driving on a road. "As a result, the fire was held to a small cost and effort," said J.F. Irwin, the supervisor of the Umatilla National Forest to the head of Varney Airlines. "Such action on the part of your flyers is very highly appreciated by forest protective organizations."

The radio telephone proved valuable on March 24, 1932, when a large gale hit Pasco, Washington, destroying a small hangar and disrupting all telephone service. Pilot Roy Warner was flying the regular westbound morning flight from Boise and informed to land at Umatilla. Meanwhile, another Varney pilot, Joe Smith, who had taken off for Pasco from Swan Island, was radioed to return to Portland after getting as far as Cascade Locks.

United Airlines

Pacific, Varney, National Air Transport, Boeing and West Coast Airlines became subsidiaries of United Airlines on March 28, 1931. From Swan Island, United Airlines observed the first interstate mail deliveries of 1912 on the twentieth anniversary of the first flight. This exact route could not be used due to postal regulations that prevented stops of this kind. The four-passenger mail ship took off from Swan Island with five thousand air mail envelopes. No landing at Pearson Field occurred, and the tri-motor plane dipped its wings as it flew over on its way to Seattle.

Nonstop passenger service from Portland to Sacramento by United began on February 27, 1933. It was a novelty. Dr. G.E. Watts, a Portland physician, flew a twin-engine Boeing monoplane owned by United Airlines to Los Angeles to attend the four days of the National Air Races on June 30, according to the *Oregonian*. United suffered its first airplane crash near Eugene, Oregon, which killed the pilot and injured a flight attendant.

During 1934 and 1935, flight delays by weather or grounding of United Airlines were covered by the news media. Also, two prominent visitors to Portland made the news by flying on United. Thomas E. Berdixen, a prominent Norwegian brewer, passed through Portland while waiting for a plane on Swan Island Airport bound for points south. Wallace Berry hunted ducks on Sauvé Island before departing Portland for San Francisco and promised to bring Clark Gable with him sometime in 1936.

The location of the first forest fire of the season was radioed on May 26, 1935, by the United Airlines pilot on the northbound flight from Los Angeles. It was observed raging in a portion of the Umpqua National Forest twenty-five miles north of Roseburg.

A grimmer story was the second United Airlines crash, which occurred six miles south of Cheyenne, Wyoming, killing four on October 30, 1935. The year ended on a lighter note when Portland florist Tommy Luke received flowers flown on the initial flight of the Pan American China Clipper from Honolulu to San Francisco via United Airlines to Portland. Oregon residents now had an air link to Asia when they flew to San Francisco.

At three months old, Merton Ferwerther became the youngest airline passenger to fly across the country in 1936. The eight-pound baby was born three months prematurely while his parents were vacationing in Oregon. A few months later, young Merton, in the care of an Oregon nurse and a United Airlines flight attendant, was delivered to his parents in Newark, New Jersey. Later in September, Martha Bjornvall, a five-year host at the Port of Portland airport at Swan Island, boarded a flight to the east for a two-week vacation.

Kathleen Norris, novelist and lecturer, returned to her California home during October after speaking on the interests of the emergency campaign on United. After three-month-old Kenneth Odgen swallowed an open safety pin, his parents drove him to Pendleton from College Place, Washington, boarding a United Airlines plane to Portland for medical help. United set two records on Christmas Eve 1936 when thirty-eight planes were in the air at the same time and a record 486 passengers flew between two cities, San Francisco and Los Angeles.

The main United Airlines news during 1937 was the return of the three Soviet polar aviators and an ambassador's departure on a chartered flight on June 22. The three aviators were escorted from a private reception at the Multnomah Hotel to the Swan Island airport, where they posed for pictures, had a radio interview with KGW and immediately departed for San Francisco and eastward to Washington, D.C.

One United flight from Seattle lost radio contact due to a PGE power outage on August 3, 1938. Departing on August 30, actress Olivia de Havilland, dressed in a two-year-old outfit with elbows peeping through, remained in the cabin of the United plane heading north to Seattle and

"Interior of Pan American Airway's Luxury Compartments." *Oregon Historical Society, folder 1059, no. 83814.*

beyond to Alberta, Canada, on a much-deserved vacation. Lora Brassfield of Tacoma, age seventy-three, climbed out of a United Airlines plane at Swan Island after her first airplane flight on October 15, 1937.

Northwest Airlines began operations connecting with Yakima, Washington, using ten-passenger Lockheed Electra airplanes on a daily schedule; it was the only other airline besides United flying out of Portland during 1938. Chicago could be reached in less than thirteen hours' flight time.

Joseph P. Kennedy, envoy to Great Britain, arrived on the United flight of January 11, 1938, for a speech covering world trade at the Masonic temple. United advertised a "fight special" to Seattle for a middle-weight title bout on July 25, 1938, with an immediate return flight to Portland.

The crew of a United Airlines northbound plane reported two small fires burning in Umpqua National Forest on May 15, 1939. Later in 1939, Eleanor Roosevelt made a ten-minute stop in Portland on October 5 while flying south from Seattle to Los Angeles. Two Portlanders—Major F.W. Leadbetter, an industrialist, and Carl Stiefel of General Motors—received membership to the Mainline Club while flying more than 100,000 miles on a scheduled airline during November 1939.

"Passengers Entering United Airlines Plane, circa 1931." *Oregon Historical Society, folder 1059.*

Alaska's flying governor, Ernst Gruening, was a momentary visitor at Swan Island, stopping for fifteen minutes on his flight from Seattle to San Francisco on August 20, 1940. Two elderly Oregonians from Salem, C.P. Bishop, age eighty-six, and his wife, boarded a United Airlines plane at Swan Island for a flight across the continent to attend the wedding of their grandson on September 26. Both United and Northwest airlines moved their flight operations from Swan Island to the new Portland-Columbia Airport on the day it was dedicated, October 13, 1940. United offered eight hundred passenger seats per day out of Portland on Douglas Commercial planes (DC-3s).

Airplane travel and stopovers by individuals still made news at the end of 1940. Ferdinand C. Smith of Merrill Lynch left December 9 on a United Airlines flight for New York City on business. Two United transports failed to land in Portland due to dense fog later that day. New York mayor Fiorello La Guardia passed through Portland on November 12, 1940, on his way north to Seattle.

The new Portland-Columbia airport became a favorite night spot on summer evenings of 1941. Every night, hundreds of people came to watch United and Northwest airlines take off and land. Spectators watched from behind the observation gates and from on top of the Northwest building observation platform. Passengers remained inside the terminals until departure time. First to board the plane was the flight attendant, followed by the pilots and passengers.

The Swan Island airport remained open for training pilots and private operations until becoming a Kaiser shipyard during early 1942. The United Terminal building, costing $2 million, was demolished in 1978 for $68,000 to make way for runway expansion of the Portland International Airport, which was completed in 1958.

BENNETT AIR TRANSPORT SERVICE

The Bennett Air Transport Service was founded by A.A. Bennett, an aviator from Fairbanks, Alaska, on August 15, 1930. Tacoma was the northern terminus of the airline. The first flights began with two Zenith biplanes carrying six passengers and a pilot south from Tacoma to the Swan Island Airport at Portland, with stops at Olympia and Chehalis.

Two Zenith passenger biplanes with a Wasp motor were added to the fleet on November 13, 1930, when regular flights were added from Portland to Coos Bay, with stops at Cottage Grove, Springfield and Corvallis.

The company became bankrupt sometime in late 1931. Bennett moved to Idaho to work as a fire patrol pilot for the federal government during the summer of 1931. By November 15, 1931, Bennett was flying mail between Boise and three Idaho mines. He remained in the aviation business as pilot and instructor at Pocatello, Idaho, until the start of the Second World War.

CHAPTER 7

HISTORICAL AIRPORTS, 1919–1942

EASTMORELAND AIRPORT

Governor Ben Olcott was the first Oregon governor to fly in an airplane. The flight took place on June 10, 1919, when the governor flew as a passenger in a Curtiss army plane from Salem, landing at the Eastmoreland municipal golf links of Portland, which at the time served as Portland's municipal airport. Seven De Havilland bombing planes commanded by Lieutenant Colonel Henry L. Watson arrived from Corvallis for the Victory Rose Festival, the first held just after the end of the Great War.

The five army planes looped and dove above Portland. From Eastmoreland Field, the planes flew with civilian passengers. "The experience of my lifetime," laughed Governor Olcott. "Here is my first adventure. All you folks, if you ever get the chance to, don't let it escape you."

Colonel R.S. Hartz, Lieutenant Leslie Arnold and Jack Harding began a 7,805-mile flight around the boundaries of the United States in a Martin bomber called the "Round the Rim Flight." The flight began on July 24, 1919, from Bolling Field at Washington, D.C. Augusta, Maine, was the first landing site. Later, the flight landed during September at Missoula, Montana and Seattle and the Eastmoreland golf course in Portland, Oregon, on October 19, 1919.

"It is only a fourth class that Portland has," said Colonel Hartz to Ray Clark of the Multnomah Hotel. "By spending $500 and putting scrapers on

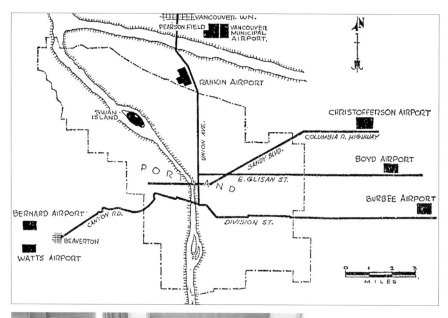

Above: "Portland Airports, May 1932." *From the* Oregonian, *May 8, 1932.*

Left: Portland Air Base pillow with an image of a Republic P-43 Lancer, circa 1940. *Photo by Murray N. Stone.*

the ground for a couple of days to make it level a fair field can be secured, but at least it can never be better than fourth-class, owing to the proximity of railroad tracks and telephone lines."

When the bomber started to taxi across the Portland field preparing for takeoff, small ridges on the ground caused the bomber to jump up and down, and it appeared as though the plane would be wrecked on the ground. The "Round the Rim Flight" left New Orleans for Washington, D.C., on November 4, 1919. The only noteworthy point of the flight for Oregon and the Pacific Northwest was the condition of Portland's landing field at Eastmoreland.

Oregon's airplane forest fire patrol began on August 9, 1919. Eight Curtiss planes landed at Eastmoreland Field from Salem. During July 1920, a forest plane reported a small fire just south of Gresham. The fire patrol aviators of the Northern Patrol moved their operations the next fire season from Eastmoreland Field to the Oregon, Washington and Idaho Aviation Field at Guild's Lake, where there were adequate machine shops.

Four pilots from Tacoma nearly crashed their planes and had to make a forced landing at Lake Oswego on May 25, 1920. The pilots failed to see the markings of the Eastmoreland Field.

SWAN ISLAND

Robert E. Byrd, the polar flyer, landed at the Rankin Field on February 13, 1927, before the Portland Municipal Airport was completed. Swan Island replaced the Eastmoreland Field just in time for Lindbergh's landing on September 14, 1927, when a pontoon bridge from the adjacent Rankin Field, which served as an automobile parking area for the event, was completed.

During 1930, four airlines operated out of Swan Island. The U.S. Weather Bureau was located on Swan Island. Weather reports from Swan Island were transmitted by radio telephone. Radio and aviation reports from Swan Island airport were popular with radio listeners on short-wave radios during the early 1930s, when AC-powered sets were available.

"To get the police and airline bulletins one must have a short-wave radio and the manufacturers of Atwater Kent Sets have introduced a ten-tube short and long wave radio combined machine," A.T. Erickson, the sales manager of Powers Furniture store, told the *Oregonian*.

Swan Island, 2024. The site of the former Portland Municipal Airport at Swan Island, where Lindbergh landed in 1927. *Photo by Murray N. Stone.*

In fact, there was a short-wave boom in Portland. The "Shorty" one-tube shortwave converter made at 2730 East Burnside offered local listeners a low-cost option. The converter has a dial scale from zero to one hundred. The setting for police was sixty, while the setting for the airport was eighty for U.S. Airline Bulletins guiding their planes and twenty-four-hour weather reports.

Passenger service ended at Swan Island in 1940 after completion of the Portland-Columbia Airport. Private planes continued to use the airport until March 1942.

POUNDER FIELD

The Cecil Pounder Field dates from 1929 and was briefly the Christofferson Field. Student Prince planes were designed by Basil B. Smith, the superintendent of Adcox School, who also instructed pilots at the Christofferson and Pounder Airports located on Northeast Sandy Boulevard east of Ninety-Sixth Avenue. The fifteen-by-two-thousand-foot-long field served as emergency site for planes of the Varney Airlines and mail planes when the Swan Island Airport was fogged in. Flying lights were installed on the field for nighttime flying operations, and a public address system was added for airshows.

The Easter air show of 1933 featured dead stick landings, upside-down flying, loops and power spins. Three airplanes and four aircraft hangars burned down in a fire on February 14, 1935.

PEARSON FIELD

The artillery grounds at Fort Vancouver, Washington, served as a testing site for Silas Christofferson during early 1910 and Alys McKey Bryant on June 12, 1913, when she set a women's altitude record. The site soon became an important airfield for aviators, including Walter Edwards, who made the first interstate airmail delivery.

The polo field of Fort Vancouver became a site for the Pacific Northwest lumber mill in the production of aviation-grade spruce lumber during World War I. The spruce was used in the construction of Curtiss JN-4 trainer and the De Havilland DH24-4 bomber used in the European Theater.

By the end of the Great War, the field was home to the 321st Observation Squadron, commanded by Oakley Kelley for six years. On September 17, 1925, with the flag raised, fifty-two army planes formed a line the length of the airfield on the Fort Vancouver parade grounds to celebrate the dedication of the airfield for Lieutenant Alexander Pearson. Pearson died after his Curtiss Racer broke apart at three hundred feet on September 2, 1924, in Dayton, Ohio, while preparing for the upcoming Pulitzer air races held during October.

Lieutenant Pearson enlisted at the start of World War I and trained at the Presidio at San Francisco and later was an instructor during the latter part of the war at Rockwell Field, California. While remaining in the U.S. Army Air Corps, he was first on time in the transcontinental Air Derby of 1921. He set a world speed record on April 1, 1923, of 169 miles per hour in a 310-mile race.

Pearson also made a record trip flying from El Paso, Texas, to Portland, Oregon, in sixteen hours, landing at the Portland Municipal Airport at Eastmoreland. He also flew down to the Grand Canyon of Arizona, mapping air currents and filming footage.

The Pearson airport was the landing site for historic flights beginning with the "Round the World Flyers" during 1924 and the Russian flyers landing there on October 19, 1929. The most famous flight, as witnessed by aviator and expert mechanic Danny Grecco, was the terminus of the first transpolar flight from Moscow by the Soviets in 1937.

In 1945, Pearson Field was decommissioned by the Army Air Corps. Today, the site serves as an airfield for the city of Vancouver, Washington.

THE WATTS FIELD

The Watts Airport was located on thirty acres of land at Beaverton, Oregon, at Erickson and Sixth Streets. The airstrip contained a one-hundred-by-two-hundred-foot building, now the Beaverton Mall. The Breeze Aircraft Corporation of San Francisco had a factory there during July 1931, as did the Pounder Company later.

Ellen Badley was the second woman to solo at Beaverton Airport and a member of the Ninety-Nines—numbered for the first ninety-nine women pilots. Her instructor's girlfriend was the first. Badley quit flying in the 1930s because a fellow student cracked up the plane, which they jointly owned, and was killed.

BERNARD FIELD

Bernard Field was the first airfield in Beaverton, dating from 1912, when Charles Bernard cleared four thousand feet of pasture and constructed a dogleg turn halfway down the hill for a turnaround for planes and motor-powered gliders. Bernard, talking like a cowboy, said, "So, I would use to take a hitch with a lariat on the airplane, snub the other end my saddle horn and go galloping down the pasture to give them enough of a boost to get off the ground. They never went very high, but they could circle around and get a good flight."

Barnard started building the first of forty wood hangars parallel to Cedar Street (now Cedar Hills Boulevard) in 1926 on thirty acres of land, featuring doors with automobile tire wheels as rollers on the bottom. The cow pasture became an emergency landing field in 1926 for the pilots flying the *Oregon Journal* newspapers to the coast. Dale and Don Holmes constructed a homebuilt glider there just north of Walker Road.

Bernard Airport/Yates Aircraft Personnel. Oil painting. *Photo by Murray N. Stone, courtesy McMenamins, Cedar Hills, Oregon.*

There were only three planes based there in 1932. Walt Rupert built a plane in 1934 that had a parasol wing and a forty-horsepower Salmon French motor that reached a top speed of one hundred miles per hour. He built two of them and sold them. In 1936, Harold Briggs set an unofficial altitude world record of 21,750 feet.

In 1938, Rupert won the National Amateur Award for the "best plane and pilot" for his Rupert Model V. George Yates built a bi-motor aircraft there in 1940. Thirty other pilots housed their homebuilt planes there.

George Yates designed and built a plane constructed of strips of spruce, crisscrossed in a basket weave pattern that may have inspired the design of the British twin-engine mosquito bomber and other wooden training planes used during World War II.

Myron "Buz" Bushwell, an Oregon Aviation Hall of Fame inductee, also learned to fly here at Bernard Field in Beaverton. He constructed homebuilt airplanes there, which was also home to the "Beaverton Outlaws."

Two Beaverton Outlaws: Charlie Bernard, George Yates. Painting. *Photo by Murray N. Stone, courtesy McMenamins, Cedar Hills, Oregon.*

In a letter to the *Oregonian*, Bernard vigorously defended the homebuilt plane industry that began in Washington County with the Long brothers. The Civil Aviation Authority, Bernard wrote in 1940, "does nothing but harm the industry. It deprives the nation of inventive ability. In no other industry is it a crime to try to make advancement."

He went on to state that the "CAA has adopted such a requirement that a private pilot cannot afford to meet them. A federal license costs next to nothing but the expense of getting it and runs several times the cost of the aircraft."

Charles Bernard was the manager in 1949, and the use of the field came to a close in 1969. It was the oldest operating airport in Oregon. The airport was demolished to make room for the Beaverton Mall, and no trace of the airfield remains. The McMenamins Pub in Cedar Mills displays pictures of the former airport.

Wood propeller, circa 1930. Above the bar on the former site of Bernards/Watts Airport.
Photo by Murray N. Stone, courtesy McMenamins, Cedar Hills, Oregon.

ALBANY MUNICIPAL AIRPORT

In operation since 1920, Albany Municipal Airport is the oldest continuously operating airport in Oregon. Charles Langmack (1907–1999) gave flying lessons there at a flight school along with his brother David. The land they rented for the flight school eventually became the Albany airport.

During 1929, the Langmack brothers bought a six-passenger plane for air service between Albany and Portland. Lieutenant Langmack trained bomber pilots in the B-17 while in the 321st Observation squadron in the Air Force Reserve, located at Pearson Field. He was a test pilot for the B-25 bomber during World War II and retired in 1967 as a colonel in the USAF after thirty-five years.

SAND POINT AIRPORT

Sand Point is a peninsula in north Seattle that runs into Lake Washington. The U.S. Navy accepted 268 acres for an airfield in 1922. On October 28, 1921, army major Henry Kress made the first military landing at Sand Point flying a Curtiss JN-4H biplane from Fort Lewis. Pilots seeded the dirt runway to give it a turf surface, but the five-hundred-foot strip turned to mud in the winter and dust in the summer.

The navy completed the first permanent hangar on August 6, 1923. The base at that time housed the U.S. Army ROTC, which had one Curtiss Jenny and six naval reserve planes. The most famous departure from Sand Point, Washington, was in 1924, when it served as the beginning and terminus for the "Around the World" flight. The takeoff was from Lake Washington to the harbor of Prince Rupert, British Columbia. Lake Washington was the center for amphibious and float plane takeoffs.

On May 11, 1925, the navy established a reserve squadron at Sand Point. The station commander and one officer worked out of a farmhouse. The supply officer ran his operation out of the kitchen. Three reserve officers assisted Lieutenant Commander J.H. Chapman and pilot instructor Lieutenant H.A. Beswick. They meet one evening per week for drills and flew every Sunday regardless of the weather.

The principal missions of Sand Point in the 1920s included the training of reservists and the aerial mapping of Washington and Alaska. By 1931, the station consisted of thirty-one full-time marines, eight naval personnel and fourteen airplanes.

In 1939, Pan American Airways began Clipper service with four-engine Sikorski S-42 flying boats. The Boeing model flying boats were first flown at Matthew's beach just north of the Sand Point Naval Station. Later, the beach became part the Sand Point station. Five active navy patrol squadrons of flying boats and six hundred sailors were assigned to the base. The runways consisted of cinder blocks paved over with asphalt.

During World War II, due to the population growth of Seattle, live bombs were loaded at the new Whidbey Island Naval Station and planes were armed for combat. There is a monument plaque of the 1924 Around the World flight at the former entrance of the Naval Air Station, now the entrance to Warren G. Magnuson Park.

La Grande

The La Grande Aircraft Company was incorporated on July 27, 1920. The company operated the airstrip at La Grande and had four planes headed by N.O. Christy. One of the pioneer pilots there was Walter E. Lees of Portland, who flew a prize Chester White Boar twenty miles from La Grande to Union, Oregon. Pilot F. Bradley and V.M. Rechstiner reached an Oregon altitude record of 16,200 feet on August 22, 1920. The passenger complained of the cold.

T.W. Baker took off from the La Grande Field to land the first plane at the new Redmond airfield, which was covered by gravel comprising red cinders from nearby Tetherow Butte. The La Grande Aircraft Company renewed its incorporation papers in 1924.

Troh's Airport

Henry Frank Troh's original airport was at the intersection of Southeast Division Street and Rockwood Road in Gresham. Troth leased land to establish a landing field for his CK biplane on a former dairy farm.

The cow barn was refitted for plane storage, and the milking room was used as a mechanic's garage. The 1,400-foot runway was a turf strip running east–west. There was a hexagonal hangar that had a windsock on the center of the roof. Troth advertised his business offering rides in his CK biplane with the slogan "Time flies, why don't you?"

Pendleton Intermediate Airfield

The sixty-acre Pendleton Intermediate field was in existence from 1928 to 1935. The grass field measured 2,640 feet from east to west and 1,320 feet from north to south. An aircraft circle marked the center of the rectangular field. There were no reported hangars in existence in 1928.

The airfield was located south of Mission Road and Purchase Lane on the Pasco to Salt Lake City airway. The Pendleton Airways School was formed in 1932 by Claude Rigden of Portland. He purchased an Aeronca-powered glider for training purposes. An air beacon, 81-by-136-foot hangar, well and heating plant were completed in 1933.

The $100,000 Pendleton Airport was dedicated on June 2, 1934. It was a regular stop of United Airlines' flights from Portland to Chicago and New York. The nonstop travel time between the Swan Island airport in Portland east to Pendleton was sixty-eight minutes. Daily round-trip flights went to Pasco, Wenatchee and Seattle. The government weather observation station at Pasco, Washington, moved to Pendleton during 1935.

The airport was occupied on September 14, 1941, with the construction of a control tower, a barbed wire fence around the airport, a bombsight storage building and 126 other buildings. Pendleton was the home base of the 17th Heavy Bomber Group, 19th Medium Bombardment Group and 89th Reconnaissance Squadron, all attached to the Northwest Air District headquarters at Spokane. Stationed at Pendleton were sixty-three B-25 bombers and 2,600 service members.

TILLAMOOK AIRFIELD

The Tillamook airfield dates from 1921, but it's had other names throughout the years. It was an emergency field with two 1,600-foot runways at the county fairgrounds. Around 1929, it became the Tillamook Municipal Airport and was operated by the American Legion Post; it had two 1,500-foot gravel runways. It was announced on June 9, 1942, that a $7 million permanent base for blimps would be located in Tillamook County. (Blimps are non-rigid directional balloons, while dirigibles are reinforced airships.)

PASCO AIRPORT

The first Pasco, Washington airport supported the airmail service of Varney Airlines. Franklin County provided funds for construction of two runways and a hangar on 160 acres of land east of Oregon Avenue and south of the cemetery, one mile southeast of the present Tri-Cities Airport. The two runways were two thousand feet long and three hundred feet wide and built for wind conditions at an acute angle to each other.

The airport was inaugurated on April 6, 1926. A bottle of grape juice was delivered by a biplane to President Coolidge since it was during Prohibition. The airport also served the mail plane service east to Elko, Nevada.

FANCHER FIELD AIRPORT

Fancher Field, as the original airfield was known, was located two miles northeast of Wenatchee, Washington. In 1930, a cancer patient was flown to San Francisco. On October 15, 1931, a Bellanca CH-400/J300 airplane, the *Miss Veedol*, flew from Misawa, Japan, making the first flight nonstop across the northern Pacific. The plane landed on one of the two oiled runways after attempts to land elsewhere at Boise, Pasco and Spokane failed due to the weather.

The aircraft had to make a belly landing at Wenatchee because the landing gear was discarded over the Pacific Ocean. The two flyers, Clyde Pangborn and Hugh Herndon, won a $25,000 prize (funded by the emperor) from the Japanese newspaper *Asahi Shimbun* for this aeronautical feat. The flight was also part of their unsuccessful attempt to break the time by Wiley Post and Harold Gatty for a flight around the world totaling eight days and sixteen hours, ending on June 1, 1931, in New York City.

BOOTH FIELD

Booth Field, later Boise's Idaho Municipal Airport, was built in 1926 and became the first hub of Varney Airlines. It was located at the south bank of the Boise River, now the campus of Boise State University. The first commercial flight passed through Boise on April 6, 1926, carrying airmail by Varney Airlines from Boise and Elko, Nevada. Charles Lindbergh landed there on September 14, 1927. During November 1931, the A.A. Bennett Air Service, with headquarters at Tacoma, began flying passengers, mail and freight from Boise to three Idaho mines.

During 1932, Booth Field had two unpaved runways in an "X" formation, along with two hangars and a terminal building painted with "Boise" on its roof on the southeast side. Varney Airlines used the 160-acre Caldwell, Idaho airport whenever Booth Field was fogged in.

Varney began operating out of Boise in 1933, later merging with National Air Transport to become United Airlines. During 1936, Boise began construction of a larger airport site four miles to the south. The new Boise airport, known as Gowen Field, opened in 1938, replacing Booth Field.

Contracts were awarded during March 1941 to pave three runways and construct drainage and lighting for the Boise airport located 4.5 miles south of town. Gowen Field was the base of the 42nd Bombardment Group, 39th Airbase Group and 16th Reconnaissance Squadron, totaling 261 officers and 1,774 enlisted air corps personnel during late 1941.

Tacoma Airport

Rudy A. Mueller and Leo H. Harkins built the first airfield in Tacoma, Washington, on the site of the old Tacoma Speedway in 1922. The first mail arrived there during 1926, delivered by a Pacific Transport Ryan M-1 plane on September 27, 1927. An office building, a parking lot and a Washington Air College hangar were also completed by Pierce County.

Robert Camwell flew a Lockheed monoplane No. 23 from Tacoma on June 19, 1928, to Felts Field at Spokane. His plane was the first of the twenty-three planes of the National Air Reliability Tour; Tacoma was the northwest hub of the tour.

Later, the Mueller-Harkins Field, located in Pierce County, became known as the Tacoma Municipal Field. A concrete runway eighty feet by two thousand feet in size was completed there during June 1929 after voter approval of a $300,000 bond measure—executed in part for Lieutenant Harold Bromley of Tacoma to attempt to fly 4,700 miles nonstop to Tokyo, Japan.

His monoplane, *City of Tacoma*, was powered by a 425-horsepower Pratt and Whitney motor and had a cruising speed of 94 miles per hour and a maximum of 115 miles per hour. The first planned flight in 1929 ended in a crash on the runway of Tacoma airport. In July 1930, flight plans was canceled due to unfavorable weather patterns and headwinds. Bromley traveled to Tokyo on September 14, 1930, for a flight over the Pacific to Tacoma, which was unsuccessful. Browley was forced to return to Japan because of a lack of fuel and gave up attempting to fly nonstop cross the Pacific Ocean.

Tacoma became the northern terminus of the Bennett Air Transport Service flights south to Portland, Springfield, and Coos Bay beginning on November 13, 1930, but this came to an end during mid-1931.

KENT AIRPORT

Herb Munter, Boeing's first test pilot, founded the original field near Seattle in 1915. The field (measuring 1,600 feet by 500 feet) and hangar served as an emergency field for the planes of the Boeing Aircraft Company. In 1920, Army Air Service planes landed and took off from there.

The 153-acre sod field near 259th and 78th was fallow until May 1928, when the Kent Flying Service began operations, dropping advertising leaflets over Kent, Washington. The three Becvar brothers—George, Charles and Lou—as well as Lloyd Armstrong, bought a surplus Jenny JN-44 and Waco 10a. Ten students attended the flight school. Two perpendicular runways, one measuring 2,000 feet northwest–southwest and the other 1,630 feet northeast–southwest, date from 1929.

The Kent School closed in 1931 due to the Great Depression. The site remained vacant until the Lynch Furniture Manufacturing Company occupied the site sometime after 1940.

CHEHALIS MUNICIPAL AIRPORT

The airport at Chehalis dates from September 1927, when A.C. John St. John painted "Chehalis" in thirteen-foot letters on his large garage, constructed a hangar and began a flying school. He bought a Ryan monoplane, a sister ship of Lindbergh's *Spirit of St. Louis*, and hired Vernon Bookwalter, a former airmail pilot, during March 1928.

Chehalis Airport was the only scheduled stop between Portland and Seattle of the West Coast Air Service, and St. John offered flights to Aberdeen and scenic flights around Mount Rainier in his Ryan Cabin monoplane. On July 20–21, 1929, Donahue Field at Chehalis was the scene of the Air Circus, comprising six army airplanes and nineteen civilian planes. During 1930, landing lights and ceiling lights were installed as advertised in the newspapers so nighttime flyers could determine the height of clouds.

The army's 91st Observation Squadron and the 3rd Balloon Squadron were stationed at Chehalis. The squadrons held maneuvers with the 3,500-men infantry troops from Fort Lewis and Fort Vancouver for three days beginning on November 21, 1939.

MINOR AIRPORTS, 1932

F.L. Burbee operated a thirty-seven-acre airfield on a tract on Southeast Division Street in Multnomah County. During 1932, the commercial field near Blair Road had two airplanes housed in new hangars. Leshe Boyd operated an airstrip on Southeast Glisan Street a half mile beyond the old KEX radio station in 1932. The private field was a base for crop dusting operations, with three airplanes.

CHAPTER 8

HELIUM-FILLED DIRIGIBLES, 1924–1934

ZEPPELIN

German aviator Prince Robert de Witte, a friend of Count Ferdinand von Zeppelin, observed the daily Los Angeles Aviation Meet of January 1911 and especially the U.S. Army balloon. He believed in the superiority of the dirigible over heavier-than-air craft.

"Germany is watching every invention closely," he said. "We have some of the French biplanes and are experimenting with them now. At the present time [1910] the [German] Army believes that the dirigible balloon is the only aircraft that can be relied upon in war."

What the German prince said was true in 1917, when German airships bombed and observed London during World War I. The American government believed that after the Great War, dirigibles could play a part in future warfare and constructed the *Shenandoah* during 1922 based on the 1917 design of the Zeppelin LZ-96.

SHENANDOAH, 1924

The dirigible *Shenandoah* entered Oregon airspace on October 17, 1924, five miles west of Brookings. The moon rose slowly from behind as the *Shenandoah* passed the mouth of the Rogue River at 9:00 p.m. Friday night. Lights twinkled along the coast, and the coastline lay white under the moonlight. The dirigible passed over Coos Bay four miles off the coast, being visible to residents. After leaving the ocean, the ship's altitude increased from 1,000 to 4,300 feet.

The radio dispatch heard on KGW radio was: "Moving slowly against the adverse wind, dirigible Shenandoah turned eastward from the Pacific over the twinkling lights of the little town of Florence, OR at 12:30 o' clock Saturday. Harrisburg was reached at 1:58, the big ship turned north to Portland. Then Corvallis at 2:25. Lights of the cities and villages showed clearly in the valley while the streams of automobiles and locomotive dotted highways and railroads on the northwest course."

A fog covered Portland as the dirigible cruised at forty miles per hour over the east side of Portland at 4:00 a.m. on October 19. It was easy to hear its passage over the city by the sound of its whirling propellers, which sounded like a small airplane. The only Portlanders to see the giant airship were observers above the fog at the top of Council Crest. The dirigible appeared in the moonlight over the eastern edge of the city as a silver object. The moonbeams reflected from the sides of the airship, bearing a silver halo of haze above.

The craft crossed the Columbia River at 4:30 a.m. on its northbound flight to Fort Lewis, Washington. Static interference prevented radio reception after the *Shenandoah* reached Kalama, Washington, at 5:15 a.m., when the first light of dawn was streaking over the Cascades and the fog turned into a purple haze.

On the return trip from its mooring mast at Fort Lewis, Washington, the 680-foot craft, refueled and replenished with helium gas, cruised north at a low elevation over Tacoma and Seattle before heading south to Oregon, passing over the mouth of the Columbia River at 5:00 p.m., clearly visible from Astoria and Seaside. The secretary of the navy responded when requests were made by radio station KGW for the *Shenandoah* to fly over Portland during its flight south to San Diego that it was a "test flight for the Shenandoah attempt to determine the capabilities of the airship and minimum time for the round trip under average conditions." In other words, Portland was not on the planned schedule. From San Diego, the great airship flew east back to its hangar at Lakehurst, New Jersey, arriving three days later. The *Shenandoah* crashed at Ava, Ohio, on September 3, 1925, with a loss of fourteen lives.

AKRON, 1931

The dirigible USS *Akron* was christened at Akron, Ohio, on August 8, 1931, and left its Pacific Coast mooring mast at Sunnyside, California, for points north on May 23, 1932, at 8:44 a.m. It took the craft two and a half hours to travel fifty-five miles north up the Pacific Coast from Gold Beach, Oregon, to Bandon due to strong headwinds. The *Akron* turned inland to Eugene and passed over Salem, where aerial photographer Burton B. Thurber met the airship in his plane flying south from Portland at 5:05 a.m., after which he began taking remarkable photos.

"The air was clear over Salem where we first saw the Akron which was beautifully silhouetted in the rising sun, slowly moving down the river," said Thurber.

The *Akron* arrived over Lake Oswego at 6:05 a.m. without a bobble at 2,000 feet. Out of the background of low-hanging white clouds at 6:15 a.m. on May 24, 1932, the 785-foot-long *Akron* suddenly appeared over the southern edge of Portland just under the clouds, bearing down the Willamette River on four of its eight 560-horsepower motors. Following the line of the west side hills, the huge craft nosed toward Swan Island Airport, at which point it turned around, passing over Sellwood before turning north on its original course.

The scattering sunrays broke through the heavy cover of clouds, playing on the silvered fabric of the *Akron* as a spotlight. The ceiling lifted. Six airplanes circled around the airship during its flight, appearing like hornets buzzing around the mammoth dirigible. Only the shafts of the propellers from its sides and the single compact control car from the lower part of the bow were visible on the 133-foot diameter of the streamlined airship.

Forty minutes later, the tail of the *Akron* disappeared down the Columbia River toward Kalama and Astoria, with its silk flag fluttering on its pointed stern between the huge elevators, fins and rudders.

One day later, the dirigible traveled north to Bellingham, Washington, before turning southward and west on the Strait of Juan de Fuca and straight south to its western base at Sunnyside, California, arriving on May 26, 1932. The *Akron* crashed on April 4, 1933, off Barnegal Lightship, New Jersey, with a loss of seventy-three lives.

MACON, 1933

The maiden flight of the dirigible *Macon* took place on April 21, 1933, at Akron, Ohio. The *Macon* was built by the Goodyear-Zeppelin Corporation for $2,450,000 and arrived at its home base on October 15, 1933, at Sunnyvale, California. On August 22, 1934, the *Macon* left its 1,118-foot-by-308-foot hangar at Sunnyvale, California, moving northward along the Pacific Coast to Grays Harbor, Washington, before turning inland to Puget Sound and Bremerton. The *Macon* cruised over Seattle for twenty-five minutes before heading south to Oregon.

Five single-seater biplanes were transported on hooks under the *Macon*. Over Vancouver, Washington, one of these planes, released from the underside of airship, was barely visible to spectators on the ground. Ten planes flew around the dirigible while it cruised at two thousand feet over Portland for the only time on August 23, 1934.

The *Macon* measured 785 feet long by 135 feet in diameter. The propellers and silvery sides of the ship reflected the brilliant rays of the sun, which was visible several miles east of Portland. The lines of the portholes were clearly visible, and it was crewed by seventy-five men.

Thirty-six thousand square yards of four-coated fabric containing aluminum powder gave the dirigible its silver sheen. The aluminum reflected instead of absorbed the heat of the sun. The lifting gas, helium, was contained in twelve separate fabric cells of varying size, made of cloth, confined and covered with layers of gelatin and latex with a covering of paraffin.

This use of nonflammable helium made the *Macon* much safer than any hydrogen-filled ship, such as the *Hindenburg*. After the *Hindenburg* disaster in 1937, there were talks in 1938 with Nazi Germany to buy helium from the United States for use in its dirigibles; this fell through due to the start of World War II.

The huge letters "US Navy" shouted from the sides of the ship. Stars indicated that it was a naval aircraft. The red, white and blue markings on the rudder and fins and the flag waving from the stern were clearly visible from the ground. By 10:30 a.m., crowds of watchers on tops of downtown Portland buildings had finally lost sight of the "Queen of the Skies" as the huge airship cruised south to Sunnyvale, California.

CHAPTER 9

LATER AVIATORS, 1925–1942

EDDIE STINSON

Eddie Stinson formed the Stinson Aircraft Company at Detroit, Michigan, in 1925. He flew over Seattle, Portland and San Francisco in early March 1928 on a "Round the Rim Flight." The purpose was to market a New Veedol oil blend, made from Pennsylvania crude oil and paraffin, for aircraft. The flight began at New York City and lasted twenty-six hours. The local distributor for this oil lubricant was the Portland Tide Water Sales office, and ads appeared in local newspapers.

Stinson landed at Medford, Oregon, and Swan Island at Portland on January 19, 1928. He was one of the thirty-one flyers who participated in the National Endurance Air Tour, reaching the Tacoma Municipal Airport; the northwest corner of the tour started from Detroit on June 30, 1928. Takeoffs at Tacoma to Spokane, Wahington were limited to times of favorable winds.

Stinson held the flight record of more than sixteen thousand hours in 1932. He died in a crash of his Stinson Model R prototype in 1932 at the Jackson Golf Course, Chicago, Illinois. He was thirty-eight years old and lived in Dearborn, Michigan.

DANIEL D. GRECCO, 1896–1983:
WITNESS TO HISTORY; LINDY AND THE RUSSIANS

Danny Grecco was an outstanding mechanic who helped assemble Silas Christofferson's plane before it flew from the top of the Multnomah Hotel to Vancouver, Washington, in 1912, as well as a participant in many other noteworthy events in Pacific Northwest aviation history. He was born in San Jose, California, and his family moved to Portland in 1904. In 1905, Danny's interest in aviation was sparked when he watched Lincoln Beachey fly a dirigible over the grounds of the Lewis and Clark Exposition.

During February 1912, he won the Meier & Frank model contest with a Curtiss Pusher. He first flew in 1913 with Christofferson aboard a Curtiss-Parker hydroplane. Then he quit high school, saving his money peddling newspapers to buy a fifty-horsepower water-cooled engine to incorporate into his homebuilt monoplane, which he flew in 1915 in a short, uncontrolled flight that scared him so much he gave up flying for three years.

Grecco joined the Army Signal Corps as a mechanic during the Great War and soloed in a JN49 Jenny powered by an OX5 engine just after the Armistice in 1918. His first parachute jump was over the Lotus Island Amusement Park on the Columbia River from the wing of a Jenny. He worked as a stunt flyer, hung from the heels from the wingtip skids and transferred from one speeding plane to another during his time with the Air Circus, headed by Tex Rankin.

In 1921, as a wing walker, he made the first transfer from a car to a plane. Another great stunt he perfected in 1925 was ascending from a speedboat going seventy miles per hour to a rope ladder hanging from a speeding airplane. One of his closest brushes with death was when he worked as a wing walker at the Tillamook County Fair. The pilot, Jack Rand, put the old Jenny into a loop, miscalculating the elevation, and while pulling out, the pilot grazed a pigpen. Luckily, they both survived this episode without a scratch.

One stunt that Grecco came up with was spoofed years later by the television series *KRPP in Cincinnati*: dropping live turkeys from a plane at Columbia Beach. Although Grecco insisted that turkeys could fly, they would be harnessed to small parachutes on Labor Day. There were many protests led by Oregon Humane Society, which threatened Grecco and the resort management with immediate arrest. Plans for the live "turkey shower" were changed by substituting dead prizes for air distribution.

"Danny Grecco." *Oregon Historical Society, folder 1059, no. 51027.*

Two passengers were killed in a plane Grecco piloted during January 1927. Later in the same year, he earned the A&E certificate and worked for the Pacific Transport Company headed by Texas Rankin and later as supervisor at the L.L. Adcox School of Airplane and Auto Mechanics at (Union) MLK Boulevard and Wasco Streets in Portland.

Grecco recalled meeting Charles Lindbergh on September 14, 1927. He was "a quiet sort of fellow. Didn't have much to say and just another pilot. Oh, sure, we all knew he had flown the Atlantic. And that that was quite a record, but everyone was trying to set records in those days, speed, altitude, endurance, distance, all kinds of records."

Lindbergh made a low pass to look over the runway. He landed on Swan Island, which was just a pile of sand heaped up from dredge spoils from the Willamette River Channel unmarked and unsurfaced, and there was no causeway connecting it to the mainland—only planks to walk across. The landing wheels of the *Spirit of St. Louis* kicked up a stick, propelling it through the fabric on the left elevator. The "Lone Eagle" only asked to see that the plane got routine inspection and servicing. Then Grecco refueled Lindy's plane and patched the hole according to instructions from Tex Rankin.

The large crowd of thousands, reported by the *Oregonian*, was never near enough to the runway to view the plane. They did not let too many on to Swan Island to see Lindbergh land. Having the landing field cordoned off, Boy Scouts were out in force to control the crowd. Lindy boarded Julius Meier's yacht for a cruise up the Willamette River to the battleship *Oregon*, anchored at downtown Portland. He made a five-minute speech on the future of aviation before thirty thousand schoolchildren at the Multnomah Stadium, stating, "We are on the verge of a great era for commercial aviation."

When three Soviet aviators landed ten years later, Grecco was there at Pearson Field, standing in front of a hangar. The Russian flyers landed in their red plane, the *Spirit of Stalin*, after flying over the North Pole from Moscow on a planned trip to Oakland, California. Their 5,288-mile flight

"Russian Fliers Landing, Vancouver, WA." *Oregon Historical Society, folder 1059.*

took sixty-three hours and twenty minutes, setting a nonstop record on June 20, 1937, and reaching a maximum elevation of sixteen thousand feet, cruising at 120 miles per hour. The aviators reached Eugene, Oregon, before turning around north to Portland because of harsh weather and having only twenty gallons of fuel remaining in the two-thousand-gallon tank.

The Russian aviators could see a large crowd assembled at Swan Island as they circled 150 feet above. Soviet flyers were familiar with Pearson Field because S.A. Shestakov landed there in a twin-engine monoplane after flying from Siberia via Attu Island, Sika and Seattle on their Round the World Flight of November 1929. Chkalov and his crew wanted to avoid the crowd that mobbed Lindbergh in Paris ten years before, so they flew north eight miles to Fort Vancouver.

Grecco recalled, "I was sitting in my Great Lakes biplane in front of the old hangar line when I saw this odd-looking bird settle down for a three-point landing and roll to a stop halfway down the field."

Harry Diamond, the chief of police for Vancouver, was patrolling Fifth Street that Sunday morning in 1937. He saw a strange-looking plane land and taxi up to the white headquarters buildings of Pearson Airport and Danny Grecco in front of a hangar door. "So, I walked up over and tried to talk to the pilots as they crawled out of the fuselage," said Chief Diamond. "They spoke a foreign language and had no identification on them. I told the soldier on guard duty to arrest them and hold them for immigration. I put them in the back of the police car and drove them up to General [George C.] Marshall's house, where Marshall said he would 'take full responsibility' for the flyers."

Chief Diamond was glad to turn over the pilot, Commander Valery Chkalov, copilot George Baldukov and navigator Alexander Bellakov because he had no authority over federal property and immigration, and the soldier refused to detain them. Diamond believed that the Russians followed him due to his police uniform, which made him appear as an official escort.

The nine-hundred-horsepower engine of the ANT25, standing for designer Andre N. Tupoler no. 25, was clean and had no oil leaks, but the cowling was black from fumes near the exhaust stacks. The engine compartments on the 110-foot-wide sail plane were padlocked to prove that it had been untouched since takeoff. Sealed barographs on the left wing provided an official record of the polar flight.

Later, Grecco helped dismantle the plane for its trip back to Moscow. He treasured a screwdriver Chkalov gave him and a rubberized cloth provision

Danny Grecco, Mr. Aviation. Oil painting. *Photo by Murray N. Stone, courtesy McMenamins, Cedar Hills, Oregon.*

sack marked in Russian "Provision No. 4, chicken breasts, sausage, butter for 3 days."

Grecco held the first commercial mechanic's license outside the Bell factory in 1947 and commuted from Portland to Yakima, Washington, to work as a helicopter instructor and mechanic. During May 1950, he joined a surveying and mapping expedition in Alaska north of Fairbanks to the Arctic Ocean, overseeing maintenance of two Bell helicopters. Beginning in 1965, Grecco and partners converted 1950s Stinson planes to seaplanes by adding floats and a new 225-horsepower Continental engine for an $8,000 conversion fee.

He was named the Outstanding Aviation Mechanic from Oregon for 1967 by the state board of aeronautics. He worked at Pearson Airpark until 1982, modifying other old aircraft and building amphibians for the Amphibians Research Company located at Pearson Air Park. He was the oldest survivor of the committee that greeted Lindbergh, passing away in 1983 at the age of eighty-six, and a participant in the main events of northwestern aviation history for more than four decades from 1912.

John G. "Tex" Rankin, 1894–1947

John G. "Tex" Rankin was born in 1894 in Brenham, Texas, hence the nickname. He started a flight school at Walla Walla in 1920, and local pilots named the airport for him. Rankin piloted a Canuck plane with Danny Grecco, performing aerobatic stunts on the wings at the Salem auto races and airplane feature on December 6, 1922.

Rankin moved his operations in 1926 to a field adjacent to Swan Island on Mocks Bottom and Union Avenue, inaugurating Portland's first air taxi service. Richard E. Byrd and Will Rogers visited the Rankin airfield in 1927.

On September 20, 1927, he entered his first transcontinental race, the Spokane Air Derby, at New York with a Waco monoplane, *City of Portland*, powered by a Wright whirlwind motor. He painted a large number "13" on his plane figuring to get national publicity, which worked, no matter how he fared in the race. Tex and his biplane were photographed and featured by the media more than any other entry in the derby. Two days later, Tex ended his flight at Lemmon, South Dakota, because of a broken cylinder rod in his motor, failing to reach Felts Field at Spokane. Newspaper headlines screamed, "Jinx 13 Catches Up with Tex Rankin."

"Tex Rankin and Mascot." *Oregon Historical Society, file 1059, no. 53579, from the* Oregonian.

Rankin advertised for a black cat to accompany as a mascot him during the National Races the next year to gain more publicity. On the designated day, nearly one hundred cat owners showed up at the Rankin Field. Rankin picked a black feline named Alba Barba, which was released by her owner.

It took several days to break the feline into aerial travel. Rankin and the cat settled in the front of the cockpit for the flight to California and eastward to New York on August 24, 1928.

The black cat was no jinx to Rankin. When he got out of the cockpit to give the kitty a sandbox break, he discovered a gas leak that put him out of the race at Columbus. "If it had not been for the cat," said Tex, "I wouldn't found that leak."

Someone stole the cat at Kansas City. Then, on September 8, someone found the cat caught in a harness in the weeds near the flying field. The mascot was shipped to the end of the race at Los Angeles, where Rankin finished fifth. After Rankin and his copilot, Walt Bohrer, spent time in Redding, California, on the trip back to Portland, the OX-5 engine overheated. Rankin did not want to fly over the Siskiyou Mountains with too heavy a load, so Bohrer had to finish the trip by bus, while the lighter-weight feline remained in the front cockpit in a harness attached to the spare magneto.

The Air Circus began with planes taking off from the New Rankin Airport west of North Union Avenue (MLK) and north of Columbia Boulevard beginning on July 29, 1928, later the site of the Portland Speedway. The Air Circus consisted of stunt flying, wing walking and parachute jumping. Air flights over Portland cost $3.50 per passenger. Three women parachute jumpers were hired that day—Rankin's private secretary, Ann "Half-Pint" Bohrer, sported a red parachute; Faye "Tiny" Carter, also from the Rankin office, was assigned a blue chute; and Dorothy Hester used a white chute.

Flying to Troutdale airport in a Ryan monoplane on May 26, 1929, Rankin evaluated a portable radio made in Portland, Oregon. The eight-tube Porta-Pak radio, weighing twelve pounds, had no external antenna and ground connection. The radio could receive radio signals despite the ignition interference from the engine. KGW came in loud and clear. Joseph Hallock of the radio firm Hallock and Watson tuned in Seattle loud and clear—it's difficult to receive on the ground in Portland during daylight hours.

Rankin flew the first nonstop "border to border" flight covering 1,350 miles from Canada to Mexico in thirteen hours, six minutes on August 12, 1929. He departed Portland to compete in the Portland to Cleveland Air Derby on August 23, 1929.

Rankin left his mark at Springfield airport just east of Eugene during the second stop of the Northwest Air Tour of 1930. Tex let his plane spin into a flying leaf and tailspin within one hundred feet of the ground. At Yakima, his propeller cracked on July 29 because of the strain of the outside loop.

At another Oregon airport, he righted the lane and cleared the plane lower than the treetops.

On February 24, 1931, he set a record of seventy-eight consecutive outside loops, and on June 26, 1932, several headlong dives under full power of the engine caused his head to ache and nose to bleed for days afterward. Rankin later surpassed his own record of 131 consecutive loops, which still stands.

Rankin discovered the value of having female students for advertising. "Flying is as much a woman's game as it is a man's game," Rankin told the *Oregonian* in 1933, praising stunt pilot Dorothy Hester and Leah Hing. "Aviation will never be a great industry until women come on par with men."

The first lesson of the Rankin School of Flying consisted of control exercises on the use of the rudder in the extremes, delivered by Rankin through a speaking tube to the student while in the air—full rudder to the left, the use of ailerons banking the airplane vertically to the left and to the right and the use of the elevators, diving and zooming the craft several times. The objective was to learn to use all three controls together to land the plane by pulling back the throttle and gliding onto the airstrip safely.

The school was closed during 1933 due to the Depression. At his school, he trained 3,500 student flyers. He moved to Los Angeles to organize a flying school at Van Nuys, California, and taught movie stars how to fly.

Rankin won the National Air Races and aerobatic championship at St. Louis on May 31, 1937. He perfected the square and upside-down outside loop. Rankin and his "Hollywood Aces" performed at Tacoma on July 22, 1939.

He left Portland during March 1941 for Tulare, California, to open his $300,000 Aeronautic Academy. The Flying Farmer airshow at Spokane was his last stunt flying event. His last commercial venture was a partnership for Republic Seabees and Ercoupe planes.

Rankin and two others died on February 23, 1947, at Klamath Falls, Oregon, while trying to avoid a residential area. After the heavily loaded plane climbed to fifty feet, suddenly, the 215-horsepower engine lost power and the four-passenger plane struck a 6,600-volt power line. "Tex" Rankin, age fifty-two, flew eleven thousand hours in his twenty-seven-year career, and in the Pacific Northwest, he is the aviator's aviator.

Lee Eyerly, 1892–1963

Lee Eyerly was born in 1892 in Cuba, Illinois. He learned to fly from Elmer Cook and bought his first airplane in 1926, a small mail plane. The Pacific Airline Service had two Waco No. 10 planes, which Eyerly flew during the September 1928 Salem State Fair. On July 27, 1929, Eyerly was injured at the Sunset Trail Air Derby at Eugene when his plane fell from a height of one hundred feet into the ground.

During 1929, Eyerly bought five acres of land with funds from the American Legion near the former governor's mansion for an airport at Salem and constructed a parasol three-seat monoplane powered by a one-hundred-horsepower motor. His *White Hen* plane was an attempt to provide a low-cost airplane in the 1930s with a Stinson four-passenger monoplane providing service between Portland, Salem, Albany and Eugene, beginning on October 11, 1930.

The Eyerly Aircraft Company incorporated on October 14, 1931, at Salem with one thousand shares. Eight Acroplanes were completed, and six were sold. Eyerly flew six hundred pounds of Oregon cherries and dressed turkeys to Denver, Colorado, in thirteen hours in 1931.

"Lee W. Eyerly and Ruth Fletcher, Salem OR, September 1930. Fleet Plane with Kinner Motor." *Oregon Historical Society, folder 1059, no. 10009.*

Eyerly won a five-lap race at the air show of the Rose Festival on June 12, 1933, piloting a Waco airplane to victory. He invented the ground-based training device the Orientator. He invented rides for carnivals like the Acroplane, Roll-O-Plane, Spider and the Octopus. He was a member of the Oregon Aeronautics Board of Aeronautics until 1958 and an inductee to the Oregon Aviation Hall of Fame.

ELREY B. JEPPESEN, 1909–1996

Elrey B. Jeppesen was from Odell, Oregon. His first flight—in a Curtiss JN-4 at age fourteen—was an eight-minute plane ride he purchased from money he made delivering newspapers and groceries. He worked with "Tex" Rankin's Flying Circus first as a ticket taker and then as a prop turner in 1924. In 1927, he soloed after only two hours and fifteen minutes in the air and later worked for Rankin as a wing walker, instructor and aerial acrobat.

Beginning in 1928, he worked for Fairchild Aerial Surveys, flying photographers and mapmakers above the Mississippi River Delta, New Orleans and Mexico in a De Havilland DH-4. He joined Boeing Air Transport in 1930 as an airline pilot and later Varney Airlines, flying the night mail. Jepp, like the other seventeen airmail pilots, had only Rand McNally road maps and the tracks of the Union Pacific Railroad to guide him when flying.

Jeppesen knew that there was a need for maps and landing field information, so he collected the drawings in a black looseleaf notebook. There was no individual event that fired him up to do all this documentation, although he had seen four aviators killed during the winter of 1930 while flying between Oakland and Cheyenne. He scouted the various airmail routes, taking photographs, climbing mountains and smokestacks, taking notes and checking out emergency fields and obstructions around them.

Finding that there was a real demand for his charts and flight manuals, he incorporated the Jeppesen Company in 1934 at Salt Lake City, Utah, selling his *Jeppesen Airway Manual* for ten dollars after the federal government expressed no interest. Today, all airlines use the manual for navigation. The Jeppesen Company became a subsidiary of Boeing Airlines in 2000.

HAROLD BROMLEY

Harold E. Bromley enlisted in the Canadian army, serving three years as a machine gunner in World War I, and later joined the British Royal Air Force. Bromley moved to Olympia and operated a flight school at Tacoma, where eighteen thousand spectators viewed his plane just before takeoff on July 28, 1929.

"I find it difficult to convince many persons that this proposed flight is not suicide," said Bromley as he boarded his plane. He carried a watch that the people of Tacoma bought for Bromley to present to the emperor of Japan.

His plane was a Lockheed Vega low wing monoplane. Bromley tried to take off from Tacoma Airport. The 904-gallon fuel tanks were overfilled so high that gas started spewing on the windshield. When Bromley leaned out the cockpit to view the problem, gasoline splatted on his googles and got into his eyes. The plane then careened off the runway, shattering the right wing and cracking the fuselage, thus ending the flight. Bromley was unhurt and vowed to try again.

The new plane was a high wing monoplane built by Emsco Aircraft of Downey, California, and transported aboard a steamship bound for Japan. On August 30, 1930, Bromley, along with navigator and radio operator Harold Gatty, started on his second flight from a naval airport near Tokyo because of the favorable tailwinds eastward toward North America and Tacoma, Washington, but the plane was too heavy to lift off. Bromley dumped fuel to lighten the load in order to avoid a clump of trees ahead of him. They were able to climb above the trees but returned to the airport because the plane lacked enough fuel to make it across the Pacific to Tacoma.

Bromley and Gatty then flew 350 miles north of Tokyo on September 14, 1930, taking off from Sabishiro Beach, a 6,800-foot beach of hard sand, lit by paper lanterns. When the pair was 1,200 miles over the Pacific and twelve hours into the flight, their exhaust system failed, and the plane became filled with fumes. Even after venting with the windows, their eyes still burned, and Bromley turned back to Japan, landing thirty-five miles north of their original starting point, where fishermen found them semiconscious from the exhaust fumes but otherwise unharmed.

The first crossing of the Pacific was achieved by Clyde Pangborn and Herb Herdon in a Bellanca CH-400/J300 airplane; it ended at Fancher Field in Wenatchee, Washington, on October 15, 1931. Nathan C. Brown on May 30, 1932, attempted to fly nonstop from Boeing Field to Tokyo but plunged one thousand feet to crash into Elliott Bay, suffering only a dislocated shoulder. Bromley then gave up trying to fly across the Pacific after the $30,000 prize money offered by a Seattle newspaper expired on June 1, 1932.

On March 29, 1933, Bromley was injured when his tri-motor transport plane crashed at Yuma, Arizona; he became known in newspapers as "Ill Luck" Bromley. He later became an American citizen and flew for Mexican mining companies, flying mail from El Paso to Mexico City and ending his aviation career as a federal aviation inspector at Oakland for twenty years. After retiring, Bromley grew grapes and dates and sold real state near his home at Palm Desert, California.

CHAPTER 10

WOMAN AVIATORS, 1926–1942

DOROTHY HESTER STENZEL, 1910–1991: "THE QUEEN OF THRILLS"

Dorothy Hester Stenzel was the "Queen of the Thrills," known for her daring acrobatics. She had her first flight at age seventeen when she borrowed the money to take a ride to Rankin Airport on Swan Island. Her instructor, Tex Rankin, called her the "Air Stunt Queen."

Rankin airfield at Swan Island was the home for the Rankin School of Flying in 1932. Among Rankin's first female students were the future stunt flyer Dorothy Hester Stenzel; the first Native American woman pilot, Mary Riddel; Leah Hing, the first female Chinese American pilot; Ann Bohrer; Faye Carter; Gladys Liedke; and nine other women.

"I believe that Dorothy Hester has already proved that woman can fly as well as men," said Rankin. "Millions of women are driving automobiles for pleasure and there is no reason why they cannot fly airplanes for pleasure."

"When I got there," Hester-Stenzel said, "the planes were all up and I thought they would run out of gas or crack up before I could get my ride."

She was the first woman in the Pacific Northwest to skydive. A pilot offered to arrange for her to make $100 for a parachute jump at the American Legion Convention in Medford. It would help her pay the $250 for flight school and another $500 for additional instruction. She was only making $0.32 per hour employed at a local woolen mill at the time as a seventeen-year-old.

Left: "Betsy Halladay in Front of Stearman CRS." *Oregon Historical Society, folder 1059, no. 47254.*

Below: "Gladys Liedel, Student, and Dorothy Hester Instructor (Right), 'The Queen of Thrills.'" *Oregon Historical Society, folder 1059, negative 60002.*

"I was hanging on the wing for dear life," she said. The pilot must have "picked up a fire extinguisher and hit me on the knuckles because I did not realize I was going on my way down."

Tex Rankin heard of her parachute jump and offered to pay her in flying hours to make jumps at his airshow on Sundays. Rankin did not support women flying at first. He later became her mentor, spending hours teaching her in an OX-5 Waco 10 biplane in which she mastered the inverted barrel roll, upside-down tail spins and outside loops.

Dorothy was the star of the Northwest Air Tour, featuring thirty-five planes during the summer of 1930 beginning at Yakima on July 29. The next day, she became the first woman to fly an airplane in an outside loop. While flying a Great Lakes biplane in 1932 with a ninety-horsepower engine, Dorothy completed five outside loops at the Grand Central Air Terminal at Glendale, California.

On May 15, 1932, she set a world record by completing fifty-six inverted snap rows at Omaha. Two days later, she executed sixty-two outside loops. Afterward, the National Air Race Officials invited her to perform in Cleveland, where she performed thirty-six death-defying stunts while flying upside down.

Ms. Hester was more afraid of crowds than stunt diving. After a performance, she would slide off the fuselage of the plane as the crowd rushed in. To get away, she hunched down low and crawled through legs, rising behind the crowd.

There was one performance where her inverted flying almost became a disaster. She was flying while a tow plane pulling four gliders entertained the crowd below. She started her flying routine and went through a series of skillful maneuvers, ending her performance with an inverted spin, unaware of what was happening around her. The tow plane was still in the air pulling the gliders over the air field. She spun through the tangle of tow ropes and the four planes and gliders, miraculously missing them all.

About her early days of flying, she said, "Flying was different back then. You could go any time you wanted, fly at any altitude, and in any kind of weather. You flew by the seat of your pants. We flew with Rand McNally Road maps. Now you must get permission before you can move your plane."

"About navigation," said Dorothy, "there was a hole in the top of the plane where you struck the sexton to get a fix and you navigated by the sun and stars."

Dorothy flew with famed aviation pioneer Wiley Post at the 1933 Ohio air show, telling her story. "When I came out of a spin he wanted out. He was so

Dorothy Hester. Oil painting. *Photo by Murray N. Stone, courtesy McMenamins, Cedar Hills, Oregon.*

sick, but the photographers wanted to take our pictures, so he let them take one. Then he ran around by the plane and threw up."

During October 1980, she was inducted to OX-5 National Aviation Pioneers Hall of Fame. Dotty was also inducted into the Oregon Aviation Hall of Fame in 2000. She holds the woman's record of sixty-two outside loops, which was set at the Omaha Air Races during mid-May 1931.

EVELYN WALDREN: "NONSTOP FLYER"

Evelyn Waldren was born in Lincoln, Nebraska. She was the first woman to receive a pilot's license in the state in 1928 at the age of nineteen. She learned to fly in a Curtiss JN-4D Jenny, a World War I trainer. In 1937, she came to Oregon from South Dakota to operate the Albany airport.

On October 1, 1941, she set the speed and distance records for a woman on a nonstop flight from Vancouver, British Columbia, to Tijuana, Mexico.

"Evelyn Waldren, Aviator." *Oregon Historical Society, folder 1059.*

She piloted a single-engine Taylor Craft for 16.5 hours, averaging one hundred miles per hour.

Waldren logged more than 23,700 hours of flight time. During World War II, she instructed army pilots. She was also a longtime instructor at Evergreen Flying Service east of Vancouver, Washington, teaching until the age of seventy-seven.

NONA MALLOY: "FLYING DRESS DESIGNER"

Nona Malloy got her start diving out of planes in Minnesota, making hundreds of parachute and wing walks. Her first jump at age seventeen came on July 1, 1926, in a plane piloted by Captain Joe Westover, a World War I ace. Nona told everyone, including Captain Westover, she was twenty-one. Jumping from 1,500 feet, she landed in a corn field that is now the site of the Minneapolis–St. Paul airport.

Her father moved to Portland from Plaza, North Dakota, and she attended Lincoln High School in Portland, Oregon, before running away at age sixteen with twenty-five dollars in her pockets, arriving in St. Paul, Minnesota. During one frightening experience when her chute ripped the airplane's wings, she braced herself against the front of the cockpit to stay alive. Fellow aviator and mentor George Badcock said before he died in a parachute jump, "You will get it sooner than later. Get out while you are ahead."

She followed Badcock's advice and abandoned parachute jumps. She had saved $500 from her time parachute jumping and used it to buy a plane, with which she hauled passengers on short excursions at the rate of one dollar per minute. Malloy and her husband moved to Portland, Oregon. After their son was born, she gave up flying for two decades. She was one of the first ten women to hold a license for parachuting, packing her own chutes and working for the Rasmussen Meadows Service at Swan Island. Later, she owned her own parachute repacking and reconditioning business during the late 1930s.

When asked how she survived stunt flying, Nona said, "I was careful. I never ever had a forced landing. Even today [1958] when I am flying the Gorge to Wasco to set down at Cascade Locks or The Dalles if the weather is bad."

She married her second husband, Dr. James D. Plamondon of Lake Oswego, in 1944 and began work as a dress designer in 1952 to support herself after Mr. Plamondon died. She remarried for a third time and returned to flying after two decades by commuting by air from Bernard Airport at Beaverton to The Dalles in her Cessna 140. She was known as the only "Flying Dress Designer" in America.

Edna Christofferson: "On Her Own"

The widow of Silas Christofferson, born Edna Bissner, became a noted aviator in her own right fifteen years after her husband died on October 31, 1916. She was the first passenger on an airplane in the Pacific Northwest when her husband placed her on top of the lower wing of a biplane flying from Vancouver to Portland on their honeymoon.

She worked as an X-ray technician in the late 1920s. She dedicated an airport for her late husband on November 1, 1931, where she learned to fly. The airport, located on Sandy Boulevard, was one mile east of Parkrose and the first Pounder Airport, where Ms. Christofferson spoke and dedicated a plaque.

After the brief ceremony, she flew solo over the one-hundred-acre airport and adjacent Inverness Golf Course dropping flowers. She was a member of the Woman's National Aeronautics Association and the Oregon Board of Aviation.

Edna Christofferson loved Alaska, flying there from Yakima, Washington, with copilot William Graham to Point Barlow, Alaska, during 1932. The pair then flew south to Nome to search for the ship *Baychimo* to salvage a cargo of $50,000 in furs, proving unsuccessful.

She stayed in Alaska for four years, owning a part interest in a gold placer mine one hundred miles north of Nome. Later, in the 1930s, she operated an X-ray school and laboratory in Vancouver, Washington, where she passed away in 1948 at the age of sixty-four. At the time of her death, she was the oldest woman flyer in the country.

EDITH FOLTZ STEARNS, 1900–1956: "THE FIRST"

Ms. Edith Foltz was the first woman in Oregon to obtain a pilot license and the fifth in the nation to secure a transport license, as well as the first to work as a commercial pilot. She first flew at the Air Derby at Corvallis on September 30, 1928. Her husband, Joseph R. Foley Jr., purchased an old army plane in 1928. She won prizes at the National Air Races for four years in a row beginning in 1929.

While living in Great Britain for three years, she ferried planes from aircraft factories to flight fields during World War II in the air transport auxiliary of the RAF. She received the King's Medal in 1946. Stearns died in 1946 at age of fifty-five in Corpus Christi, Texas.

ALYS MCKEY BRYANT, 1880–1954: "HIGH FLYER"

Alys McKey Bryant was born on August 28, 1880, in rural Indiana. She was the first woman to fly on the Pacific Coast, having begun flying in 1912. She worked for the Fred Bennett Aero team in California and

Oregon, along with brothers Milton and Frank Bryant, flying at Boise, Idaho, and Baker City, Oregon.

Her first paid exhibition flight took place in Yakima, Washington, on May 3, 1913, during which she flew to Baker City on May 31. She was a member of the Early Birds of Aviation, an organization for aviators who soloed prior to December 17, 1916.

The gray-eyed McKey set an altitude record of 2,800 feet over the Columbia River on June 13, 1913, the cross-country record for a woman flyer in the Pacific Northwest. She married her instructor, John Milton Bryant, who later died in an airplane crash at Victoria, British Columbia, on August 6, 1913.

When asked about being afraid of flying, she said, "I believe you die but once no matter where you are." Her greatest fear instead was of exhibition crowds, which she compared to wolves who "almost tear off the clothes of a flyer who has been hurt in order to give souvenirs."

In 1915, Alys married maritime engineer Jessie W. Callow in Seattle. She worked as a professional deep-sea diver and trained pilots during World War I, living to be seventy-three.

NANCY KISTER: THE "FORCED LANDING QUEEN"

Nancy Kister flew solo after seven hours of instruction from Tex Rankin's Flying Service at the age of sixteen. She became a minor celebrity when she took off from Swan Island heading east toward the Columbia River Gorge; the engine of the Jenny died, but she landed safely. Luckily for her, there was an open pasture near Troutdale, where she landed without any mishap. Soon thereafter, a farmer ran out to greet her; he checked out the plane and discovered that there was no gas in the tanks.

"I am so sorry," said Nancy. "I have no money to pay for the crop damage or for any gasoline." The pasture owner told her not to worry and invited her to join him and his wife for lunch. Miss Kister wondered what she could do to make things right because the couple was so understanding. The farmer noted her unease and said, "How about giving me a ride in that flying machine so I can have a look from up in the air and wave to my neighbors?"

The young woman was hesitant because she had no right to haul a passenger after only one solo flight. Nancy decided that there was nothing else for her to do, so the farmer agreed to buy some gas and fill the tanks. He hopped aboard, and they flew from his farm over the neighbors' homes.

Her next flight took her from Swan Island to the Interstate Bridge on the Columbia River to Pearson Field at Vancouver, Washington. Everything went according to plan until she could not gain the necessary altitude to leap over the bridge. Then she decided to fly *under* the bridge, which was not a wise decision because the Columbia River at this time of year was at flood stage and there was little space between the water and the bottom span of the bridge.

She began her maneuver with only inches to spare on all sides. Somehow guided by instinct, Nancy made it through flying blind; however, the spinning propeller sucked up water from the river's surface and dumped it all back into the cockpit. She held her course and pulled back on the stick just in time to clear the bridge, later arriving at the Pearson Field looking like a drowned cat.

The outcomes of her next three flights were always the same. She had no difficulties in taking off, but a short time later, the plane's engines sputtered and died because of lack of fuel. She discovered that the other pilots were draining her gas tank so they could fly a little longer. From that point on, Kister started checking her gas tank before every flight and earned the respect of other pilots as the "Forced Landing Queen of the Northwest."

LEAH HING, 1907–2001: THE FIRST OF HER ANCESTRY

Leah Hing took her first airplane ride around the time she was playing saxophone for the Portland Chinese Girls Orchestra in Chicago in 1930. During 1934, she obtained her pilot's license at Tex Rankin's flying school, soloing in a Great Lakes training biplane over Union Avenue and the Rankin airfield. She was born in Portland, Oregon, and became the first Chinese American woman to gain a pilot's license.

"It is a great sport," said Leah. "I believe that woman can learn to fly as well as men and eventually there will be just as many women flying as men. Someday, I hope to be able to teach other Chinese woman to fly."

In 1936, Hing bought her own plane, a 1931 Fleet Model 2, taking off from Portland and Pearson Field in Vancouver, Washington, with many private passengers. Later, she bought a Wright-powered Traveler open

"Leah Hing, First Chinese-American Woman Pilot." *Oregon Historical Society No. 58757.*

three-seat plane from Dorothy Hester Hofer. Leah joined the Ninety-Nines in 1939 and was secretary-treasurer of the Northwest Chapter in 1941. The Ninety-Nines organization was founded by Amelia Earhart in 1929 for the first ninety-nine women to receive federal private pilot licenses; it promoted flying among women and sought to train civilian pilots. During World War II, Hing worked with the West Coast Civil Air Patrol doing ground training and repairing navigational instruments at the Portland Air Base.

She let her pilot's license expire in 1947 and explained later that she was not anxious to fly again and just "enjoyed flying as a passenger." Hing was employed at the Aero Club of Portland as a hat checker, switchboard operator, receptionist and photographer until retiring at seventy in 1977.

CHAPTER 11

AVIATORS IN THE FIGHT, 1942

THE OREGON FLYING TIGER

Kenneth Jernstedt was born in Yamhill County in 1917 and grew up on a farm near Carton. He graduated from Yamhill High School in 1935 and from Linfield College in January 1939. He enlisted in the U.S. Marine Corps in 1941, becoming Oregon's only member of the Flying Tigers when he resigned his Marine Corps commission with the secret approval of the U.S. government.

He joined the Flying Tigers because he "knew of atrocities and had great empathy for China," as he related in 1995 in the *Oregonian*. "We were young, well trained, and hungry for adventure. I went with two buddies and we kind of talked each other into it."

The Flying Tigers arrived in China during April 1941 and first saw combat on December 20, 1941. Jernstedt was a part of the dawn raid on Moulmein Airport. He was flight leader of the Third Squadron, with thirty aircraft. He destroyed twelve Japanese aircraft, becoming a Double Ace while flying the Curtiss P-40.

Jernstedt accompanied flight leader William Norman Reed and strafed two airfields, being credited with destroying fifteen Japanese aircraft on the ground, splitting a bonus of $7,500 (about $500 per plane). Later, he destroyed three additional planes.

"US Navy Goodyear Blimp, Circa 1942. James Mulkay, Crew Member." *Oregon Historical Society, folder 1059, no. 26452.*

After contracting dengue fever while on duty in Asia, he was confined to a McMinnville, Oregon hospital for a week ending July 30, 1942. Afterward, he worked as a test pilot for Republic Aircraft Company, based on Long Island, New York, after the Flying Tigers disbanded.

The public airport at Hood River Airport along with the gates to the Portland National Guard Base were named in his honor on September 6, 2001.

THE DOOLITTLE FLYERS

The 17th Bomb Group at McCord Field, Washington, was transferred to South Carolina during February 1942. The bomber group had been selected to train at the Columbia Army Airbase for the upcoming Doolittle Raid on Tokyo, Japan.

The eighty-man raid occurred on April 18, 1942, leaving the aircraft carrier *Hornet*. Three Oregon aviators accompanied Colonel James Doolittle. They were Master Sergeant Jacob D. Deshazer, age twenty-nine, of Madras; Lieutenant Robert S. Clever; and Second Lieutenant Dean

Anderson. Only one Boeing B-25 bomber avoided crashing by landing at an airbase near Vladivostok in the USSR. Seventy-three raiders eventually returned to the United States.

The bombers came in at twenty feet above sea level, sweeping over the paddy fields and pagodas. The crews were astonished when farmers waved hats and handkerchiefs while they flew over. The civilians thought that the aircraft were Japanese planes.

The 17th Bombardment Group flew anti-submarine aircraft from Pendleton, Oregon, after being moved cross-country to the Columbia Army Airbase at West Columbia, South Carolina. Corporal Jacob D. Deshazer from Salem, Oregon, was a bombardier and a POW for forty months, returning to United States on September 4, 1945.

Lieutenant Anderson, age twenty-two, of Portland graduated from the Air Corps Advanced Training at Stockton, California. He received the Flying Cross and Silver Star as a pilot due to his actions during the air raid on Tokyo. He was on furlough and returned to active on July 20, 1942. Lieutenant Clever, who was the bombardier on Anderson's flight, died in a bomber plane clash in the United States during November 1942.

Captain Charles R. Greening, a pilot from Tacoma, Washington, invented the "Mark Twain," the seven-inch-square low-altitude bombsight fitting in the Norden frame used by the Doolittle raiders. Captain Greening and aviator crews also patrolled the Oregon coast for Japanese submarines, taking off from Pendleton Field with depth charges.

Japan released hundreds of fake submarines consisting of a float and a fake periscope in their attempt to tie up antisubmarine spotter plane efforts. There were 147 reported submarine sightings during December 1941 and 1942, but some were only Japanese decoys.

SUBMARINES

The submarine threat was real. The Japanese had eight long-distance I-class submarines patrolling off the Pacific Coast, with a range of twenty-two thousand nautical miles. The 17th Bombardment Group at McCord Field near Tacoma was equipped with the Douglas B-18 Bolo bomber and the B-25 Mitchell bomber. On December 14, 1941, a B-25 medium bomber station at McCord Field dropped four bombs on a Japanese submarine, *I-25*, near the mouth of the Columbia River.

These submarines had a 5.5-inch deck gun for shelling. Another sub, the *I-17*, opened fire with its deck gun off Santa Barbara, California, on February 23, 1942. This was the only American site shelled by an enemy nation since the War of 1812.

Three Japanese submarines were able to stalk Pacific Northwest waters: the *I-5* off Cape Blanco, the *I-26* at the entrance of the Strait of Juan de Fuca and the *I-25* at the mouth of the Columbia River. The home base of the dirigible *Tillie*, F photo section or aerial reconnaissance and the IX observation squadrons was at Gray Field at Fort Lewis, Washington. The *I-25* fired a torpedo at the SS *Connecticut*, hitting the port side on December 27, 1941, and also fired against Battery Russell at Fort Stevens on June 21, 1942.

Submarines carried a Yokosuka E-14-Y1 Glen float plane in their deck hangars, used for reconnaissance and which was launched by catapult. The *I-25* returned for its second campaign, leaving Japan on August 15, 1942. The Glen had a range of nine hundred miles and was equipped with two incendiary bombs intended to start forest fires.

Captain Jean Daugherty, on patrol in a Lockheed A29 Hudson bomber from McCord Army Airfield at Tacoma, Washington, came across something dark in the water ahead of them while flying through a fog bank. It seemed larger than the pictures of the Japanese submarines shown at briefings.

"Suddenly we broke into the bright sunlight," said Captain Daugherty. "I throttled back to reduce speed, lost more altitude, and headed straight toward the long, low, object." Then they opened the bay doors.

The bombardier dropped a few three-hundred-pound bombs, missing the submarine. However, the two bombs rattled the *I-25*, forcing it to settle on the sea bottom at Port Orford Harbor to evade detection. On the evening of September 29, 1942, the Glen dropped two bombs onto Grassy Knob, east of Port Orford, but these did not produce any damage.

Western Oregon and Washington State provided a countryside similar to western Europe, proving valuable for training American flyers. The clear skies east of the Cascade Mountains provided good flying weather throughout the region.

The U.S. Navy used Moon Island, Washington, and the Clatsop County Airport in Warrington for seaplane patrols on the Pacific coastline. The naval station at Tongue Point, where groundbreaking occurred in 1939, was not operational until late 1942.

ALEUTIAN ISLAND CAMPAIGN

Lieutenant Charles E. Perkins spotted a Japanese aircraft carrier on the first day of the Japanese attack on Dutch Harbor on June 3, 1942, and another at the nearby army station at Fort Meyers, also on the Aleutian island of Unalaska. Five waves of three enemy planes came out of the clouds at 6:00 a.m. during the twenty-minute attack, which occurred at the same time as the Japanese attack on Midway Island two thousand miles to the south. A second attack occurred the next day with eighteen Japanese carrier-based airplanes.

Charles E. Perkins and his crew flew over a Japanese carrier on June 3, 1942; it was escorting a cruiser and opened fire on an American PBY. After the airplane engine quit, the American pilot and crew were forced to fly with only one motor. "I dropped my load of bombs at 8,000 feet and headed the craft toward the base, said Lieutenant Lucius Campbell. "However, our fuel gave out and we were forced to make a landing on the sea. The Coast Guard rescued us."

Albert C. Knack, a machinist mate from Portland, Oregon, aboard a Catalina flying boat, bombed a Japanese transport near the fog-covered island of Kiska on June 5, 1942. This was first American plane to score a direct hit on a Japanese vessel.

U.S. Army Liberator bombers based on the islands blasted the Japanese submarine base on Kiska Island and shore installations beginning on October 8, 1942. The Aleutian Islands of Attu and Kiska, six hundred miles east of Dutch Harbor on Unalaska Island, were liberated by the U.S. Armed Forces by 1943.

OREGON AVIATION HONOR ROLL NOMINEES

John Connor Burkhart

Main Criteria
1. Natural-born citizen: Albany, Oregon, 1883; active in aviation from 1908 to November 1918.
2. Enlisted as a captain in U.S. Army Air Corps, October 1917–December 1918; member, War Production Board.
3. Designed and piloted a double-rudder biplane, flying over Portland, Oregon, in 1913 and added a hydroplane attachment; associate editor, *Aeronautics* magazine (1911).

Outstanding Achievements Aviation
1. Flying techniques: trial and error; first flight, August 1908, Cornell University.
2. Aircraft design: lateral control by wing lengthening/shortening and hydroplane.
3. Fixed base of operation: Goltra Park, Albany, Oregon, and O.K. Jeffery County, Portland, Oregon.
4. Aviation promotion: the second man to fly a plane in Oregon just one month after Charles Hamilton, *Oregonian*, March 23, 1910, 11; appearance and exhibit at Portland air show, January 22–31, 1910.
5. Military achievements and assignments: captain, U.S. Army Air Corps, 1917–November 1918.
6. Education: mechanical engineering degree from Cornell University, 1909, New York.

Essential Information

1. Solo: Cornell University, August 1908. First aviator to build and fly an owner-built airplane constructed in the state of Oregon, March 23, 1910, letter to the editor by William C. Crawford, *Oregonian*, January 20, 1933; perfected aircraft's unique steering system, making four flights during September 1912 over Albany and Portland, Oregon.
2. Aircraft experience: designed airplane having unique system of lateral control by both lengthening top wing and shortening the other tip at the same time; designed hydroplane for O.K. Jeffery Manufacturing Company, Portland, Oregon, during 1914.
3. Aviation employment: self-employed mechanic, 1910–13; chief designer and engineer for O.K. Jeffery Manufacturing, Portland, 1914–September 1917; captain, U.S. Army Air Corps, October 1917–December 1918.
4. Awards and recognition: President Herbert Hoover radio address, May 23, 1931, for Cornell University War Memorial. Note: Burkhart is listed, as he died in World War I.

Louis Barin

Main Criteria

1. Natural-born citizen: Davenport, Iowa.
2. Instructor: U.S. Navy at Pensacola, Florida.
3. Designed and piloted pontoon takeoffs, Portland, Oregon, 1914–17.
4. Flying techniques: Curtiss flying school.
5. Aircraft design: flying boats.
6. Fixed base of operation: Portland, Oregon, 1914–17; Pensacola, Florida, 1917–19; San Diego, California, 1920.
7. Aviation promotion: test pilot, air races, exhibitions and aerial navigator.
8. Military achievements and assignments: navigator on May 1919 navy plane flight to the Azores.
9. Education: trained by John C. Burkhart, who built the first plane in Oregon.

Essential Information

1. Solo: Portland, Oregon, 1914.
2. Aircraft experience: test pilot, air races, naval navigator and exhibitions with Curtiss biplanes.

3. Aviation employment: test pilot for John Burkhart, 1914–17; U.S. Navy instructor, 1917–20.
4. Awards and recognition: navigator on U.S. Navy/Curtiss NC-1, first attempt to cross the Atlantic by way of Azores, May 1919; San Diego airshow, 1920.

Eugene Ely

Main Criteria
1. Natural-born citizen: Williamsburg, Iowa, October 21, 1886.
2. Enlisted: U.S. Navy.
3. First airplane takeoff and landings on U.S. warships.

Outstanding Aviation Achievements
1. Fixed base of operation: Portland, Oregon, 1910; San Francisco 1911.
2. Aviation promotion in Oregon: airshows at Portland Rose Festival and Salem.
3. First takeoff from a warship, the USS *Birmingham*, anchored in Chesapeake Bay, flying onto a landing on a dry beach in Virginia, November 14, 1911. First landing on a warship, the USS *Pennsylvania*, in San Francisco Bay, January 18, 1912.

Essential Information
1. Solo: accidental takeoff at Rose City Racetrack, Portland, Oregon, April 10, 1910.
2. Aircraft experience: Curtiss biplane Model D, Hudson River Flyer, Curtiss Racer.
3. Aviation employment: Auburn Automobile Service; Glenn Curtiss organization, pilot and sales; U.S. Navy, pilot, instructor, appointed aviation instructor for Coast Artillery Corps.
4. Awards and recognition: U.S. Navy, Distinguished Flying Cross (posthumously).
5. Sources: *Oregonian*, *Oregon Journal*, Oregon Historical Society, Wikipedia and the internet.

Silas Christofferson

Main Criteria

1. Natural-born citizen: Des Moines, Iowa, 1890.
2. First interstate flight: June 6, 1911.
3. Employed by U.S. Navy, 1914.
4. Outstanding achievements: flew from the roof of Multnomah Hotel to Vancouver, Washington, June 11, 1912.
5. Fixed base of operations: Vancouver, Washington, and Portland, Oregon; moved to Redwood City, California, 1913–16.
6. Air Derby, Portland, June 1914: flew over and under three Willamette River bridges.
7. Military assignments: bombed USS *South Dakota* with sandbags, September 24, 1914, showing aircraft's role in future warfare.
8. Aviation ratings: pilot license.
9. Aeronautical education: Curtiss Flying School, San Francisco, California, 1912.

Essential Information

1. Solo: homebuilt monoplane at the artillery grounds, Fort Vancouver, Washington, 1910.
2. Aircraft experience: Curtiss Flyers; converted Curtiss biplane by adding pontoon and two floats, making a hydroplane, July 1912; piloted T.S. Baldwin's plane *Red Devil* during January 1913; flew Racine biplane over Mount Whitney, California, on June 23, 1914, setting U.S. altitude record; also set long-distance record flying Racine biplane 310 miles from San Francisco to Bakersfield, California.
3. Aviation employment: Bennett-Christofferson Air Ship Company, 1910–12; Christofferson Aircraft of Oregon, 1912–13; Christofferson Company, Redwood City, California, 1913–16.
4. Recognition: set U.S. altitude and long-distance records, June 23, 1914.
5. Sources: *Oregonian*, *Oregon Journal* newspaper archives, Wikipedia and the internet.

Walter Edwards

Main Criteria
1. Natural-born citizen: New York City, 1880.
2. Employed: Bennett Aero Company, 1912.
3. Outstanding achievements: made first official interstate U.S. mail delivery, August 12, 1912.

Outstanding Aviation Achievements
1. Carried 1,500 pieces of mail on August 12, 1912, from Portland, Oregon, to Vancouver, Washington.
2. Flew Curtiss airplane and hydroplanes.
3. Fixed base of operation: Portland, Oregon, and Willamette River south to Oregon City.

Essential Information
1. Solo: early 1912.
2. Aircraft experience: Curtiss Jenny, Pusher style; piloting hydroplanes; Thomas Baldwin's plane, *Red Devil.*
3. Aircraft employment: Bennett Aero Company, 1912; Claude Berlin; Thomas S. Baldwin.
4. Rewards and recognition: first interstate mail delivery, Portland, Oregon, to Vancouver, Washington, August 12, 1912; hydroplane altitude record of two thousand feet, Portland, Oregon, August 4, 1912.
5. Sources: *Oregonian, Oregon Journal* newspaper archives, Wikipedia and the internet.

Charles Walsh

Main Criteria
1. Natural-born citizen: Mission Valley, California, October 27, 1877.
3. Employed: Pacific Aircraft Company, Portland, Oregon, May 1, 1911–September 29, 1911; Curtiss Exhibition flyer, August 31, 1911–October 1912, headquartered at Hammondsport, New York.
4. Flying techniques: Curtiss school at San Diego, California.
5. Solo: Imperial Beach, California, April 10, 1910.

OUTSTANDING AVIATION ACHIEVEMENTS

1. American altitude record of 7,200 feet at Laramie, Wyoming, July 7, 1911.
2. Fixed base of operations: San Diego, California, 1909–11; Portland, Oregon, and Vancouver, Washington, during 1911; Curtiss Exhibition team, late September 1911–October 2, 1912.
3. Aircraft design: Curtiss Silver Dart, Curtiss-Farman biplane.

BIBLIOGRAPHY

Introduction

Chanute, Octave. *Recent Progress in Aviation*. *Scientific American* supplement. New York: Munn & Company, 1910.

Harris, Patrick. "The Exhibition Era of Early Aviation." *Oregon Historical Society* (Fall 1986): 245–76.

Milbank, Jeremiah, Jr. *The First Century of Flight in America*. Princeton, NJ: Princeton University Press, 1943.

"A Splendid Spectacle." *Oregonian*, October 30, 1866, 3. Reprint, October 30, 1916, 8.

Wellman, Walter. *The Aerial Age*. New York: A.R. Keller and Company, 1910.

Chapter 1: The Civil War Era, 1861–1882

"Advertisement." *Oregonian*, November 9, 1889, 5.

"Aerial Department." *Oregonian*, January 20, 1862, 2.

"Aeronaut's Accident." *Oregonian*, May 11, 1890.

"Aeroplane Almost Ready for Trial." *Oregon Journal*, June 28, 1904, 2.

"Aged Man Trifles with Air." *Oregonian*, October 24, 1909, 8.

"Another Parachute Jump." *Oregonian*, November 10, 1889, 8.

"Ballooning for the Army." *Oregonian*, July 4, 1861, 2.

"Beautiful Balloon Ascension." *Oregonian*, November 6, 1883, 3.

"Devoured by Sharks." *Oregonian*, November 24, 1889, 1.

"Did He Commit Suicide." *Oregonian*, August 13, 1890, 8.

"Eddie Should Have Milked Cows." *Oregonian*, February 4, 1959, 1.

"Gala Day at the Park." *Oregonian*, April 14, 1890, 7.

"Gas Bag Ascension." Ad, *Oregonian*, 1888, 4.

"The Great Airship." *Oregonian*, November 11, 1888, 8.

"He Landed in the River." *Oregonian*, September 12, 1889, 18.

"Ho! For the Clouds." *Oregonian*, January 9, 1898, 4.

"It's Been 75 Years Since Powered Flight Was Born." *Oregon Journal*, December 14, 1978, 119.

Milbank, Jeremiah, Jr. *The First Century of Flight in America*. Princeton, NJ: Princeton University Press, 1943.

Oregonian. P.H. Redmond and Eddie Hall story, 1889, 12.

"Professor Redmond, the Aeronaut." *Oregonian*, June 1, 1890, 6.

"Repairs His Balloon." *Oregonian*, September 30, 1888, 5.

"A Ride in a Balloon to Salem." Ad, *Oregonian*, September 23, 1888, 4, 5.

"Salem Notes." *Oregonian*, September 26, 1883, 3.

"Up in a Balloon Boys." *Oregonian*, September 24, 1888, 8.

"Van Tassell Ascends at Last but His Wife Did Not Make the Great Parachute Jump." *Oregonian*, October 15, 1888, 8.

"Van Tassell's Lost Balloon." *Oregonian*, September 26, 1888, 3.

"Van Tassell Usual Bad Luck." *Oregonian*, October 6, 1888, 5.

"Van Tassell Will Try Again." *Oregonian*, September 28, 1888, 8.

"Veteran Balloonist at Chehalis." *Oregonian*, June 29, 1913, 3.

"Walla Walla Skydiver of 1900s." *Oregonian*, March 17, 1963, 117.

"Will Navigate the Heavens." *East Oregonian*, June 23, 1904, 1.

"Yesterday, Balloon Ascension." *Oregonian*, November 11, 1889, 6.

Chapter 2: The Balloon Era, 1882–1895

"As It Looks from Here." *Oregonian*, Magazine Section, September 18, 1949, 15.

"Balloon Survived." *Oregonian*, February 2, 1959, 9.

Bartholomew, Robert E. "From Airships to Flying Saucers." *Oregon Historical Quarterly* 101, no. 2 (2000): 193–201.

"Dream of Former Days of La Grande Resident Realized." *Oregon Journal*, August 22, 1920, 11.

"An Oakland Airship." *Oregonian*, November 29, 1896, 2.

"Portland Man Has Solved the Great Problem." *Oregonian*, November 10, 1900, 7.

Spitzer, Paul G. "Stock in Flight: The Arrival of Aviation in Oregon." *Oregon Historical Society* 91, no. 4 (1990): 371–77.

"War's Aeronautics." *Oregonian*, January 7, 1894, 10.

Chapter 3: Failed Dreams and Hoaxes, 1895–1904

"Captain J.W. Kern Dead." *Oregonian*, June 29, 1900, 8.

"Captain J.W. Kern: To Travel in the Air." *Oregonian*, January 12, 1896, 9.

"East Side Affairs." *Oregonian*, July 6, 1900, 8.

"Here Is an Airship." *Oregonian*, December 27, 1896, 8.

"Kerns Range Finder." *Oregonian*, September 15, 1899, 8.

Chapter 4: Dirigibles, 1905–1910

"Airship Again Is King of the Air." *Oregonian*, August 22, 1905, 8.

"Airship Angelus Flies Over Oregon City." *Oregonian*, July 19, 1905, 1.

"Airship Company Incorporated." *Oregonian*, January 29, 1910, 9.

"Airship Made New Record." *Oregon Journal*, September 15, 1905, 1.

"Day of All Days at Exposition." *Oregonian*, September 30, 1905, 1, 10.

"Flight of Airship." *Oregonian*, August 26, 1905, 10.

"Great Airship Under Construction at Exposition Grounds." *Oregonian*, November 7, 1909, 8.

"His Record Flight in Air." *Oregonian*, September 10, 1905, 8.

Maddux, Percy. *City on the Willamette: The Story of Portland, Oregon*. Portland, OR: Binfords & Mort, 1952.

"Makes Best Flight." *Oregonian*, September 16, 1905, 10.

"New Airship's Great Flight." *Oregonian*, August 20, 1905, 8.

"Prepare for Maiden Trip." *Oregon Journal*, October 18, 1909, 1, 3.

"Rekar Airship Frame." January 3, 1910, 12.

"Terrific Gale Hits Pasco." *Oregon Journal*, March 24, 1932, 1, 2.

"Varney Pilot Spots Forest Fire." *Oregon Journal*, September 2, 1931, 15.

"Visitors May Inspect Balloon." *Oregon Journal*, June 4, 1910, 4.

Chapter 5: The Aviators, 1910–1924

"Air Full of Plans to Make Airships." *Oregonian*, January 30, 1910, 10.

"Airplane Equilibrator Test." *Oregonian*, June 30, 1911, 13.

"Airship Crashes as Tailless Kite." *Oregonian*, June 9, 1911, 6.

"Airship Mail Man Soars Over City." *Oregonian*, August 4, 1912, 1, 14.

"Albany." *Oregon Journal*, July 23, 1914, 17.

"Aviation Corps of Naval Militia Being Formed." *Oregon Journal*, November 12, 1915, 13.

"Aviator Bombard Seattle." *Seattle Times*, July 19, 1914, 2.

"Aviator Flies a Bit on Parade Grounds South of Barracks." *Vancouver (WA) Columbian*, June 13, 1911, 5.

"Aviator Hamilton Dies." *Oregonian*, January 23, 1914, 3.

"Aviator Making Flights at Country Club." *Oregon Journal*, May 28, 1911, 11.

"Aviator Much Hurt." *Oregonian*, August 13, 1910, 2.

"Aviator Walsh Killed." *Oregonian*, October 4, 1912, 5.

"Aviator Will Fly." *Oregonian*, March 10, 1913, 10.

"Aviator Will Try Again." *Oregonian*, May 20, 1910, 5.

"Big Airship Plans Progress." *Oregonian*, February 23, 1910, 15.

"Birdman Is at Albany." *Oregonian*, May 24, 1912, 1, 8.

"Bomb Strikes War Ship." *Oregonian*, November 23, 1913, 33.

"Burkhart Determined to Perfect Airplane." *Oregonian*, March 13, 1910, 10.

"Burkhart Falls with Aeroplane." *Oregonian*, March 10, 1910, 1.

"Burkhart Flies Over Portland." *Oregonian*, April 12, 1913, 18.

"Burkhart Machine Falls." *Oregonian*, April 19, 1910, 7, 10.

"Burkhart's Craft Flies." *Oregonian*, March 23, 1910, 11.

"Burkhart Will Fly Again." *Oregonian*, March 15, 1910, 9.

"Cachet Flight Planned." *Oregonian*, August 10, 1932, 8.

"Christofferson, Prophet Who Sprouted Wings." *Oregonian*, NW Section, October 26, 1941, 3.

"City Pays Tribute to World Aviators." *Oregonian*, October 18, 1924, 1, 6.

"Daring Aviator Makes Thrilling Flight in Safety." *Oregon Journal*, June 12, 1911, 8.

"Device Aids Flight." *Oregonian*, August 6, 1911, 7.

"Device to Help Airplane." *Oregonian*, June 26, 1911, 11.

"Dream of a Former La Grande Resident Realized." *Oregon Journal*, August 22, 1920, 11.

Ellsworth, Dighton B. U.S. Patent 1024398A, "Equilibrator for Airship." December 12, 1910.

"Ely Flight Delayed." *Oregonian*, October 11, 1910, 4.

"Ely in Aeroplane Lands on Warship." *Oregonian*, January 19, 1911, 3.

"Ely Is First in Aeroplane Race." *Oregonian*, December 28, 1910, 1, 3.

"Ely Is Upset in Wemme Aeroplane." April 14, 1910, 15.

"Eugene Ely Killed." *Oregonian*, October 20, 1911, 1, 4.

"Even Aviators Are Worried About Tires." *Oregonian*, November 2, 1919, 8.

"1500 Pieces Go by Air Route." *Oregonian*, August 14, 1912, 1, 14, 16.

"Flight Easily Made." *Oregonian*, March 22, 1910, 8.

"Flight from Ship Is Great Success." *Oregonian*, November 5, 1910, 3.

"Flight in Air Is Made by Accident." *Oregonian*, April 13, 1910, 1.

"Flights Are Guaranteed." *Oregonian*, March 10, 1910, 12.

"Hamilton Flies Swiftly." *Oregonian*, March 15, 1912, 1.

"Hamilton Thrills Crowd." *Oregonian*, March 6, 1910, 1, 8.

"J.C. Burkhart Returns." *Oregonian*, August 5, 1917, 28.

"John Burkhart, First Oregon Plane Builder." *Oregonian*, Magazine Section, April 27, 1947, 1.

"La Grande Aviators, Reach 16,200 Feet." *Oregon Journal*, August 23, 1920, 11.

"New Air Record Sought." *Oregonian*, July 15, 1930, 19.

"New Airship Tried." *Oregonian*, April 28, 1911, 9.

"Oregon Early Day Aeronautics." *Oregonian*, June 1, 1969, 14.

"Pioneers Work Recognized." *Oregonian*, October 25, 1931, 19.

"Plane Plant Opens Spruce Parts for Army Flyers." *Oregonian*, August 1, 1917, 6.

"Portland Aviator Flies with Ease." *Oregonian*, April 10, 1910, 7.

"Portlander Was Pilot for Villa." *Oregon Journal*, December 2, 1977, 13.

"Portland Man Will Fly." *Oregonian*, January 2, 1912, 7.

"Portland to See Aero Planes Today." *Oregonian*, March 5, 1910, 12.

"Seibel Has Pluck." *Oregonian*, August 14, 1910, 11.

"Sky Craft Draw Curious Throng." January 25, 1910, 1, 4.

"Sutherlin to Be Scene of Aviation Meeting." *Oregon Journal*, March 20, 1910, 40.

"Teaching the Fine Art of Warfare." *Oregonian*, February 9, 1913, 8.

Thomas, Lowell. "Flying Around the World." *Oregonian*, December 2, 1924, 12; December 14, 1924, 20; February 4, 1925, 16; February 6, 1925, 17.

"Throng Pays Loud Acclaim to Air Heroes at Eugene." *Oregon Journal*, October 18, 1924, 1, 12.

"Trial Flight Is Success." *Oregonian*, April 17, 1910, 29.

"Two Aero-planes Ready for Show." *Oregonian*, January 22, 1910, 18.

"Walsh Sails Over Part of East Side." *Oregon Journal*, May 23, 1911, 16.
"Walsh Smashes His Airplane." *Oregonian*, January 24, 1910, 4.
"World Aviators Guests at Banquet." *Oregonian*, October 29, 1924, 2.

Chapter 6: Aviation Companies

"Air Firm Elects." *Oregonian*, February 12, 1927, 2.
"Air Mail Flight Out of Portland." *Oregonian*, October 26, 1927, 6, 7.
"Air Mail Job Wanted." *Oregonian*, May 20, 1920, 6.
"Air Man in City." *Oregonian*, February 18, 1926, 6.
"Air Transport Incorporated." *Oregonian*, January 9, 1926, 8.
"Big Air Line to Celebrate." *Oregonian*, August 18, 1941, 7.
"Five Oregon Airplane Manufacturers." *Western Flying* (1929).
"News Item." *Oregonian*, March 19, 1926, 11.
Redman, Art. "The Legacy of Leslie W. Long." *Call Letter*, August 2008, 10–11.
———. "Leslie Long: The Airplane Years." *Call Letter*, July 2007.
"Those Who Come and Go." *Oregonian*, October 10, 1919, 10.
"World Greatest Airplane Factory to Be at Seattle." *Oregon Journal*, December 16, 1928, 1, 3.
"Worldwide Industry Rises from Modest Oregon Farm." *Oregonian*, Section 6, July 31, 1934, 4.

Chapter 7: Historical Airports, 1919–1942

"Aviation Radio Station Here to Go on the Air Soon." *Oregon Journal*, September 1929, 54.
"Beaverton's Busiest Pasture." *Oregonian*, November 20, 1955, 119.
"Federal Policy Menaces Progress." *Oregonian*, April 14, 1940, 24.
"Harold Bromley, Aviator Lacking Lindbergh's Luck, Dies at 99." *New York Times*, Section 1, Jan. 11, 1998, 28.
"Lights to Mark Route." *Oregonian*, June 9, 1926, 2.
"New Airport to Open at Pendleton." *Oregonian*, June 1, 1934, 6.
Redman, Art. "Short Wave Boom." *Call Letter*, April 2019, 7, 8.
"Tacoma Airport Graded." *Oregonian*, May 22, 1929, 18.
"2000 View Dedication of Airport." *Oregonian*, October 14, 1940, 1, 8.
"US Readies Return of Airfield to Towns." *Oregonian*, November 15, 1945, 9.

Chapter 8: Helium-Filled Dirigibles, 1924–1934

"Akron Passes Over Portland." *Oregonian*, May 25, 1932, 1, 4.

"Famed Navy Flyer Staunch for Dirigibles." *Oregonian*, October 28, 1933, 3.

"Flying Levitation Gives City Thrill." *Oregonian*, August 24, 1934, 1, 2.

"Navy Answer Protest." *Oregonian*, October 21, 1924, 6.

"Portland Sees Macon." *Oregonian*, August 24, 1934, 1, 2.

"Shenandoah Passes Over as City Slumbers." *Oregonian*, October 19, 1924, 1, 4, 10.

Chapter 9: Later Aviators, 1925–1942

"Adcox School Gets Govt. Ratting." *Oregonian*, March 20, 1932, 10.

"Air Circus All Ready." *Oregonian*, October 6, 1928, 2.

"Al Set for Boat Races." *Oregonian*, August 7, 1925, 12.

"Crash Dashes Flyers Hope for Hop." *Oregon Journal*, May 31, 1932, 10.

"The Eagle of the World Drops from the Sky to Receive Portlanders." *Oregonian*, September 15, 1927, 10, 11.

"Grecco to Join Adcox." *Oregonian*, February 27, 1930, 15.

"Lee Eyerly Corporation Starts Air Service." *Oregon Journal*, October 11, 1930, 9.

"Mechanic Recalls Lindy Just Another Pilot." *Oregonian*, August 31, 1977, 47.

"Obituary." *Oregonian*, October 15, 1983, 26.

"Oregon Products Featured." *Oregon Journal*, September 18, 1929, 2.

"Plane Hits Power Line at Klamath." *Oregonian*, February 24, 1947, 1, 9.

"Planes that Can't Fly." *Oregonian*, Magazine Section, January 31, 1954, 95, 96.

"Police of Chief Recalls Landing of Soviets." *Oregonian*, July 17, 1987, 29.

"Rankin Off to Try Non-Stop Border Flight." *Oregon Journal*, August 11, 1929, 7.

"Tex Rankin Acts as Host of Radio Part." *Oregonian*, May 26, 1929, 51.

"35-Year Veteran Named Top Aviation Mechanic." *Oregonian*, December 23, 1967, 13.

"Veehol." Oil ad, *Oregonian*, March 25, 1928, 70.

Chapter 10: Woman Aviators, 1926–1942

"Airborne Dress Designer Smitten by Flying at Age 4." *Oregonian*, June 1, 1958, 60.

"Aviation Pioneer Recalls Jump into Stunt Career." *Oregonian*, July 20, 1981, 15.

"Aviator and Diver Too." *Oregon Journal*, Section 2, January 7, 1917, 8.

"Chinese Girl Flying Pupil Quick to Acquire Knack." *Oregonian*, March 6, 1932, 52.

Gildemeister, Jerry. *Avian Dreamers*. Limited ed. printing. La Grande, OR: Bear Hollow, 1991.

"Old Time Woman Pilots, Relieve Pioneer Days." *Oregon Journal*, November 6, 1974, 26.

Oregon Hall of Aviation. "Evelyn Burson." Oregon Aviation Historical Society. https://oregonaviation.org.

"Woman Spends 45 Years in Air." *Oregon Journal*, August 13, 1973, 18.

Chapter 11: Aviators in the Fight, 1942

"Boise Medium Bombers." *Oregonian*, April 6, 1941, 66.

"Naval Flyers Tell of Flight." *Oregon Journal*, September 8, 1942, 6.

Nelson, Kurt R. *Fighting for Paradise: A Military History of the Pacific Northwest*. Yarley, PA: Westholme Publishing, 2007, 249–60.

"Oregon's Flying Tiger." *Oregonian*, Magazine Section, July 5, 1942, 6.

"Oregon's Flying Tiger Gains Acclaiming of China for Jap Hits." *Oregon Journal*, Magazine Section, April 5, 1945, D-5.

"Weather Big Aleut Factor." *Oregonian*, August 28, 1942, 5.

ABOUT THE AUTHOR

The author lives in Portland, Oregon. He has written more than sixty historical (nonfiction stories) articles for *Oregon Coast Magazine*, *Antique Radio Classified*, *Call Letter*, *Lost Treasure*, *Treasure Cache*, *World War II* and *Eastern/Western Treasure*. This is his second historical book on Oregon. The first was *Oregon Lost Treasures*. This book covers the history of flight from the beginning of the American Civil War in 1861, when *Oregonian*s were involved, to the start of World War II during 1942—relating the story of flight in Oregon and Washington to the history of aviation of the United States.

Visit us at
www.historypress.com